SONGBYRD
Becoming She

SONGBYRD
Becoming She

the memoir of
Caisie Breen

Published by
Songbyrd Publishing
Portland, OR

Published by Songbyrd Publishing
PO BOX 30075
Portland, OR 97294

ISBN: 0692820078

ISBN-13: 978-0692820070

Cover design by Margot Boland
Interior design & layout by Benjie Nelson
Editing by Jess Clarson

This is a work of creative nonfiction. The events are portrayed
to the best of Caisie Breen's memory. While all the stories in
this book are true, some names and identifying details have
been changed to protect the privacy of the people involved.

Printed in the United States of America

In loving Memory of
Grace Harpole

ACKNOWLEDGMENTS

I want to thank all those who were part of my journey to Becoming She.

Thanks to the wonderful women of WEO, (Women Entrepreneurs of Oregon), for taking me in while still male, and calling me one of their own. They showed me the love and acceptance that ultimately allowed me to come out and be authentic; She! And a special thank you to Tia Ribary, of WEO, who opened my eyes.

Thank you to Patty Myers from Success Group International, for making me feel welcome during my awkward coming out at our contractor's convention and graciously accepting me into their women's group.

Thank you to Diane Hanson and Martine Barnett for welcoming me as a hostess for Jockey clothes for Women, and hosted home parties for me.

Thank you to my wonderful staff at Casey's Plumbing and Metro's Best Electric for making me feel free to be me in an environment that often misunderstands my community.

Thank you to my first writing coach, Eva Hunter. Eva taught me the basics of writing and got me started with my memoir. I also want to thank my second writing coach, Stacy Pershall from Gotham University, who helped me bring my manuscript to completion.

Thank you to my daughter-in-law, Jess Clarson, for her priceless help with editing and proof reading.

Thank you to Margot Boland for her excellent work designing the book cover and thank you to Benjie Nelson for the interior design.

Thank you to those in my Facebook group—Songbyrd, who help me navigate my never-ending search for new sound.

Thank you to my friend Jenny Boylan, for her selfless, and almost always behind the scenes, examples of helping others in our community. It was such benevolence that got my attention early on, and inspired me to seek her out for some personal counsel. And of course, I was inspired by Jenny's, writing—particularly, "I'm Looking Through You."

And of course, I thank those in my family who support me and indeed, stood by me from the beginning.

Most of all, I thank my lovely wife—my Brenda Sweet. For without her, the world would never have met, Caisie Breen.

CHAPTER ONE

"I want to be her."

I pointed to the skinny girl on the cover of an *AdvoCare* diet magazine. I couldn't believe I said it—not only once, but twice. I was in Portland, Oregon, at the home of my sales rep Penny, picking up a new order of products. Pushing fifty and becoming very self-conscious about my weight, I was selling diet products to save money on my orders.

Penny was taken aback. "Don't we all want to be that skinny?"

"No, I want to *be* her!"

Penny had a troubled look on her face as we exchanged goodbyes. When I got in my car, I was embarrassed and almost went back to apologize. What was I thinking? My comment surprised me as much as it surprised her. I decided to forget about it and hoped she would, too.

This was a horrible thing to happen to a conservative Republican like me. I opposed gay rights and had campaigned against them in an Oregon referendum, strongly supporting religious "traditional values." And yet, a feminine side was seeping into my life—some of it consciously, some not. I decided I wasn't going to tell my wife, whom I affectionately called "Brenda Sweet," what I'd said.

Our two boys, Ryan and Brandon, were still in grade school. Our home was a light yellow, two-story, remodeled Cape Cod in the suburbs with a large yard and a white picket fence.

When I got home, our dog Rachel ran to my car, barking. She was a golden retriever mix, just large enough to knock someone down if she was excited. She was excited.

"Oh Rachel, Rachel. No—down, down!" I laughed as she tried to lick me into forgetting that she'd escaped from the house. I took her inside and had a talk with my son about keeping her indoors.

"Hi, honey. What's up?" I asked as I plopped myself into our sofa chair.

"Weekenders," Brenda answered. "Don't you remember? I have seven women coming, and they'll be here in an hour. I'm afraid you're going to have to make yourself scarce and leave for a couple of hours, or stay in the back. If you stay here, you'll have to be invisible—they'll be changing in the living room and bathrooms."

Weekenders was a home-based party plan for selling casual women's clothes. "Oh that's right," I said. "I forgot. I'm going to hang out in the back."

Brenda's women's clothing shows enticed me. I occasionally used women's clothes during sex as an enhancement. Before our boys were born, we would explore gender role-playing at our favorite weekend beach getaway in Lincoln City. We always made a stop at the local thrift store to check out soft and silky undergarments to liven things up. One weekend had really gotten crazy.

"Hey hun," I'd said. "Check out the black stockings over in the markdowns. There are even some matching garter belts in there. Will you get them for me, please?" I was too timid to grab them myself.

"Sure," Brenda said with a giggle.

I stood in the men's aisle next to the bin of stockings, watching Brenda's every move and becoming overheated. Fantasizing about what our evening would look like lowered my inhibitions.

I left the men's aisle and slowly walked up behind Brenda. She was still slightly bent over, rummaging around in the large bin full of stockings and wigs. I placed my hands on her shoulders and gently moved my pelvis up against her butt. I did my best to keep my movements discreet, but I was euphoric and didn't care if someone saw me pawing my wife.

I pressed my pelvis a little harder.

"Oh my God. You're driving me crazy," Brenda said.

"That's the plan, my Brenda Sweet. I'm all yours tonight!" I whispered, slowly grinding.

"Oo, oo, oo! Yes, you are. You're mine tonight! And you're going to do anything I say, right?"

"Absolutely, sweetie. No questions asked. Absolutely," I said like a well-trained puppy dog.

By the time we left the store, I was feeling softer and more feminine than I had in years. The motel was only minutes away, and when we walked through the front door, I said, "Okay, babe, will you do me up with makeup tonight? I want to be pretty."

"Really? Okay, sit right here." She pointed to a small table next to the bathroom. "Now, I'm going to put a little eyeliner on you."

She applied a thin stroke of eyeliner at the base of my eyelashes, and then continued applying makeup to the rest of my face. With each stroke of a brush, I felt a delightful zing.

"There. Oh my. Go look in the mirror, honey," said Brenda.

I looked in the mirror and saw that she was right—I was gorgeous! In my head I was singing "Walk on the Wild Side": "Plucked her eyebrows on the way/Shaved her legs and then he was a she/She said, hey, babe, take a walk on the wild side/ Said, hey, honey, take a walk on the wild side."

"So what do you think?" Brenda asked.

"Come here, my Brenda Sweet," I said. "I'll show you what I think."

We spent the next hour having sex, playing lesbian lovers. Brenda and I were both beautiful and so in love. We embraced and kissed until I exploded in total bliss, which immediately dissolved into feelings of guilt and shame.

"I need to get this shit off my face, now," I said as I ran to the bathroom. From the time I was at the thrift store to the time I climaxed, I had felt feminine and beautiful, but now I just felt ashamed. This struggle wasn't new, and it wasn't the last time it would happen.

And now I found myself wanting to be part of Brenda's Weekenders party. But what an insane thought—to be a *part* of it? *What was I thinking?* This wasn't a sex game, playing femme. This was a women's clothing party.

"Okay, Bill. I need your help," Brenda said. "Will you get the card table and set it here against the dining table? And we need snacks. Can you fix us a veggie tray, sweetie?"

"Sure. I'll get right on it," I replied.

Just as I put the veggies out, the first party guest arrived.

"Oh you. Shoo, shoo," Brenda said to me. "Time to make yourself scarce — and thank you, honey, for all your help." She gave me a big kiss.

I went to my hideout at the rear of the house, kicked back, and began reading my paperback, *Anne of Green Gables*. As Brenda's party guests arrived, I couldn't help listening in on the conversation and fun.

"Oh look, Brenda!" said one of the party guests. "This is exactly what I wanted at your last party, but you were out. And they even have it in green!"

"I know, Diane. And check this out. The Little Red Dress!" Brenda said.

"I want, I want! My goodness, Brenda, that'll look gorgeous on you. It's the exact same cut as last year's Little Black Dress. I've got to have one," Diane said.

I felt a strong urge to go out and see some of the clothes everyone was so excited about. After all, my male wardrobe consisted of just four pairs of jeans, all blue, and five or six short-sleeved shirts.

Just before I peeped out the door, Brenda came rushing in with an armload of clothes to try on.

"Hi, honey. Both bathrooms are occupied, and I need to try on this Little Red Dress." She pulled her top off, slid out of her pants, and had that pretty little dress on in less than sixty seconds. She held her arms out to the side and asked, "How do I look, honey?"

"Wow! Dangerous as hell. Seriously, it looks gorgeous on you," I said, laying my book down.

"Aww, thanks, sweetie." Brenda kissed my cheek, put her clothes back on, and rushed back to the party, leaving the Little Red Dress behind. I grabbed it, held it up against my chest, and looked at myself in the full-length mirror. I felt a lump in my throat as I saw how beautiful I was.

I slowly laid the dress down across a chair. Bill Casey, beautiful? How could I look so wonderful and yet feel so dirty? I felt a sense of loss as I listened to the girls giggle and talk about the clothes. It seemed that there was such camaraderie with women, whereas in my male world, I always felt I was in competition. When I was younger, it was either who played the best sports or chugged beer the fastest, and as adults, it was who made the highest sales among our employees. These women were talking about each other's families, current dress styles, makeup, and color combinations. I longed to be included, but that wasn't to be—not at that party, anyway.

After the last woman left, my Brenda Sweet came back to get me. "Hi, honey. You can come out now. Everyone's gone."

"How'd you do?" I asked.

"Pretty good. Everyone bought at least one catalogue item. And how about you? Did you get lonely back here by yourself?"

"'You know, honey," I said. "I know this sounds weird, but I found myself wanting to be part of your party. I heard you all having such a good time."

Brenda smiled her sweet smile. "I understand. Of course you would want to be a part of it—we had a blast. But there were women changing clothes; you know it wouldn't work."

I wanted her to understand. "That's the crazy thing, dear. I began imagining myself trying on those clothes with everyone else. And there wasn't anything sexual about it at all. I could see myself going through the different colors and styles, trying on what I liked, like everyone else, and it felt great; it felt natural. I know. Weird, huh?"

"Wow. That's a leap, all right." Brenda thought for a moment. "Tell you what. Why don't we do a little dress-up party occasionally here at home for you, and see what happens? If this is something you want, I'll see what I can do about future parties."

What an amazing and confusing thing: a politically conservative anti-gay cross-dresser. But if anyone had told me then that I was transgender, I'd have dismissed the thought. Not me! I just wanted to do girly things once in a while.

Holding that dress up to my body in the mirror caused me to recall a much earlier day of dress-up. I'd kind of forgotten the incident when I was five, with my sister's cute pink dress.

CHAPTER TWO

"Come on, baby
Let's do the twist
Come on, baby
Let's do the twist…
Yeah, you should see my little sis
You should see my little sis
She really knows how to rock
She knows how to twist"

By the age of five, I had developed an unusually keen taste for music. One particular spring afternoon, I heard a ruckus from my sister Valerie's room that sounded a lot like a popular song I'd heard on the radio, along with some loud squeaking sounds.

We lived in an older two-story house with three bedrooms. My sister's room was on the main floor next to the kitchen, and her single bed was in the center of the room. Grandma Grace was in the kitchen preparing food for that evening's dinner. I loved the song I was hearing but couldn't figure out what the other noise was. I ran into Valerie's room, and there she was, jumping up and down on her bed, swinging and swaying to the music playing on her transistor radio. Her bed had gigantic coil springs that made loud creaks and squeaks with every one of her gleeful crash landings. The noise got louder as my sister's energy level increased and her jumps got higher.

"Hey Billie, here—put this on," Valerie said, and she threw me one of her dresses. It was light pink, and I was particularly fond of that color. So I tossed my shirt and trousers, slid the dress over my Jockey underwear, and joined her as we both danced to "The Twist" on the bed. I didn't feel at all unusual in my sister's dress, and it flew up and down with every jump I made. I was, in fact, comfortable, and I loved how it felt as it touched my skin with every bounce.

The culture at that time, however, had very strict ideas for what little boys and girls should wear and how they should behave. And as a young boy, getting caught in a pink dress could be considered a family crisis at worst, or an opportunity for a good sit-down talk at best.

I certainly wasn't aware of any such taboos, but my fun came to a halt when my grandmother walked into the room with an expression of bewilderment and fear. Just that unfamiliar look on her face caused an empty feeling in my heart.

"Billie!" she scolded. "Take that dress off at once and put your own clothes back on. Don't you ever do this sort of thing again. And really, Valerie, what were you thinking anyway, letting him wear one of your dresses?"

Even though Grandma Grace put a stop to my early girly experience, we remained close. Whether it was letting me help in preparing meals or just taking the time to talk, Grandma Grace was always there for me.

"Billie, c'mon Billie. Time to get up. Today's your first day of school, and you don't want to be late," said Grandma Grace.

"Oh yeah," I said, rubbing my eyes.

"And your mom will be taking you. She got back home last night."

My mother was a professional singer and did a lot of traveling with her band.

"Oh boy. Mom!" I said, running to the kitchen.

"Mom."

"Well, hello, Billie. You'd better eat your breakfast. We need to get you to school. This is your first day. Are you excited?" said Mom.

"Oh. I guess so," I replied.

Mom took me to school and introduced me to my first-grade teacher.

"Hello, are you Mrs. Martine?" asked Mom.

"Yes. And you must be Mrs. Casey. And this must be Billie. Glad to meet you. You can pick him up this afternoon at 2:30."

"Will do, Mrs. Martine, and thank you," said Mom.

I got along with the little girls much better than I did with the boys.

In the classroom, the girls were in a corner cutting out magazine pictures and pasting them on paper. Meanwhile, the boys colored on blank pieces of paper. I joined the girls.

"Hi, Patty. What are you making?" I asked.

"I'm making my family. See, there's my mother, my dad, my sister, my cat, and I'm going to color in my yard now."

"Billie. Billie, please get back to your seat. I do believe you may be girl crazy!" said Mrs. Martine.

On the playground, most of the boys were out in the field, playing ball, while several girls did their best to get some speed from the cold, steel merry-go-round. I loved trying to get it up to speeds that would make everyone dizzy.

"Billie, push me! I want to go faster. Go, push faster, faster, faster!" screamed one of the girls riding.

"Let's go. Jump on now!" I yelled to two more girls thinking about joining the ride. But my glee turned to fear as one of the girls fell off and the teacher heard her scream.

"Billie! What have you done?" asked Mrs. Martine. "Why aren't you playing with the boys out in the field? See, they're playing ball. Now get out there and play with them. You're too rough for the girls. She consoled the crying girl in a way she hadn't consoled me when I'd fallen off the merry-go-round during morning recess. Nobody said anything to the girl doing the pushing then. And I had no interest in playing ball. I walked away with my head down and stood by the school entrance until recess was over. My first day was off to a rocky start, and I watched the clock the rest of the afternoon, looking forward to my ride home with Mom.

"Okay, Billie. Let's go," said Mom after the dismissal bell rang. She took my hand as we walked to her car.

"Well, how was your first day at school, Billie? Did you make any friends?" asked Mom as she started the car.

"It was okay," I said. I didn't tell her about the incident on the playground.

When we got home, Grandma was already in the kitchen preparing our dinner.

"Hi, Grandma. Whatcha doing?" I asked.

"Same as usual. Fixing dinner."

"And how was your first day at school?" she asked.

"Awe, not that great. My teacher got mad at me for playing with the girls."

"That's odd. Why would that make her mad? You weren't being mean, were you?"

"No. But when a girl fell off the merry-go-round, Mrs. Martine got mad and told me to go play with the boys."

"Tell you what. I'm about to make some cookies for dessert. Wanna help?"

"Yes!" I said gleefully.

Grandma was a short, plump woman in her seventies, still with some brown color to her hair. We spent the next hour cutting out sugar cookies and had them in the oven before dinner. After we ate, my mother needed to get ready for work. As a professional singer, she did her makeup a little brighter than most women. I watched her methodically apply it in our small 1950s bathroom. She stood over the small, porcelain, wall-hung sink as she looked into the narrow, wall-mounted, medicine-cabinet mirror. I was enthralled, watching her squint as she applied glitter eye shadow.

"Hey, Mom. What's that?" I asked.

"That's my eye shadow, honey," she said.

"It's so pretty."

And then she would smile and start singing one of her songs as I continued to watch in fascination.

She was always an animated woman, and from the time I was old enough to start school, she seemed to value my opinion about what she wore. Given the many parties and events she sang for; she was always looking for something special.

"Billie," she'd ask, holding up a couple of dresses. "Which one do you like?"

"Oh, I like the red one, Mom," I'd almost always say. "It's so beautiful!"

It didn't matter which dress she held up next to her red-sequined dress. Eventually, she caught on that the red dress would always be my choice, but continued to ask anyway—with a wink.

Her second husband was a bass player named Johnny Skiles, and they performed and traveled together. This was the pinnacle of her musical career. She had cut at least one record, a song called "Cole Miner," and she performed on *The Louisiana Hayride* TV show. That show kick-started Elvis Presley's career. One week, she sang "Bee Bop a Lula" on *American Bandstand.*

The morning after that performance, I walked down the hall toward my first-grade class, and some of the teachers stuck their heads out to greet me, saying things like, "Hey, Billie! We saw your mother on *American Bandstand* last night. She was really cool!"

Cool? Cool indeed! Inside I was thinking, *Um, okay, so what?* The only music I considered cool was the Beatles. Of course, to appear on *American Bandstand* was something all striving musicians longed for—an opportunity to display their talents all over America. Even the Beatles performed "Strawberry Fields" on the show in 1967. I was too young to appreciate the significance of her appearance.

We moved to a newer, single story house within blocks of my school. It was large enough for my mother to have her friends over for her occasional practice jam sessions. And I did appreciate all the attention I received during those sessions.

One evening when she was partying with her friends, she sat me next to her on the piano bench and sang to me. She was in a gleeful mood, smiling down, singing a song I think she made up on the spot—"And when I go out, I go with Billie, cause Billie knows just where to go…" The rest of her band joined in on a performance that seemed tailored for me. Men seemed to fall at her feet in those days.

Those early days of music and partying were exciting, but over time, they became routine—just a way of life. And although I never learned to sing or play an instrument, I did become an avid connoisseur of music. In fact, when I discovered that there were actually people in the world who weren't as moved by music as I was, I started using the term "music people" to describe myself and others like me. We needed music in our daily lives, in our triumphs and challenges. There was always a song that would express my feelings, motivate me when I needed a push, excite me when I needed to celebrate, and—too many times—cry for me when all seemed lost.

CHAPTER THREE

In 1964, I was nine, the Beatles were the rage, and everywhere I went — the school bus, the playground, everywhere—I heard people singing, "She loves you, yeah, yeah, yeah!" and "I wanna hold your hand." Even the adults. It was a wonderfully crazy time for music people.

> *"Oh yeah,*
> *I'll tell you something,*
> *I think you'll understand.*
> *When I say that something,*
> *I wanna hold your hand!*
> *I wanna hold your hand.*
> *I wanna hold your hand."*

The Beatles electrified America with their music, and thus the term "Beatlemania" was coined. As the '60s music scene continued to grow, I would occasionally listen to other artists, but most of my friends considered me a "narrow-minded Beatles freak." I was hooked, head over heels in love.

At Sunnyside Elementary School, I had a good friend named Ted. He came over one afternoon to play and listen to my mother and her musician friends. My mother sang the blues.

Ted considered my house a cool hangout because of the hip music and lingo. He was always amazed when I would drop something like "groovy" or "far out, man!" on him.

"Hey, Ted, let's like, check out some of my mom's 45s," I said.

"Wow! Where did you come up with those words? You know, 'like,' 'groovy' and 'far out'?" said Ted.

"I don't know, Ted; I just talk like I talk."

"Wow, so cool!" he replied.

It wasn't long before Ted and other kids at school picked up on some of that "cool lingo." He and I were great pals—until the day we got into a fistfight. He thought I had said something offensive and began pushing me.

"Hey, man. C'mon. Put 'em up!" he yelled.

"I don't know what you're talking about. I didn't say anything," I replied.

That didn't dissuade him, and the fight was on! After jabbing each other several times, he grabbed my left arm, gave it a good twist and a pull, and *snap*. I let out a scream so loud that it sent all the neighbor kids running, including Ted.

My mother wasn't home and Grandma didn't drive, so getting to the doctor could have meant an ambulance, which would have embarrassed me terribly. Fortunately, a kind neighbor witnessed everything and volunteered to help. She rushed me to a local doctor's office, where they X-rayed my arm. Sure enough, it was broken.

The X-ray revealed an existing unicameral bone cyst covering most of the upper humerus of my left arm. *I just loved those big words, "upper humerus."* The cyst had eaten so much of the bone that it was honeycombed and brittle.

I was in luck though, because there was a Shriners Hospital for Crippled Children in town. They took on young children like me with parents who couldn't afford such an operation. The hospital was a beautiful, white, two-story building with smaller wings attached diagonally at each end. The building itself was set high on a huge, lush green acreage, and the grounds were decorated with colorful bushes and flowers. Occasionally, on a sunny day, it was a little utopia for many of the bedridden children. The nurses' aides, who wore pink-and-white candy-striped uniforms, wheeled them out in their beds and wheelchairs to take in the fresh air and enjoy the warmth of the sun.

When I was admitted, they placed me in the boys' ward, at the opposite end of the hallway from the girls'. The boys' ward had the color and style of the fifties —the beds had light-green metal frames with pull-up side rails. Shriners was a well laid out and disciplined hospital, but I found ways to entertain myself.

One of my friends was a twelve-year-old named Martin, who was paralyzed from the waist down, which required him to wear a metal halo attached to a bar that went all the way down his back. They said he had a curved spine and that the bar would eventually straighten it. Even though his mobility was restricted to only arm and finger movements, he made the best of what he had.

Like me, Martin loved rock music, and he had a battery-powered transistor radio about the size of an egg carton attached to the bar over his bed. He played that radio for most of the day, and he loved when "Purple Haze" by Jimi Hendrix came on. We all became spellbound; I imagined him wheeling his guitar behind his back, jumping up and down without missing a beat, and plucking the strings with his teeth, like he did in live concerts. There were many other artists we rocked to—like the Beatles, of course; the Turtles; and the Rolling Stones. But for Martin, it had to be Hendrix.

I woke up one Saturday morning feeling full of energy, and because it was warm and bright outside, I knew the staff would move a third of the beds outside so the patients could see the sun. And because it was a weekend, the radio would be screaming with my favorite tunes.

"Hey Martin, are you going outside after breakfast?" I said.

"Heck no! The acoustics are terrible out there, and with so many kids gone, we can crank it up!"

"Cool! I was hoping you'd say that. After breakfast they'll be heading out while we rock!" The food carts came in with hot oatmeal and fruit. For many, it was better than they had at home and certainly more consistent. By the time the cleanup carts cleared away the trays, several kids had fallen asleep. That didn't deter the candy stripers from taking them out into the sun anyway. Unless a person was awake enough to tell the staff that he or she planned on remaining indoors, that person was wheeled out with everyone else.

"Okay, Martin, let's see how clear KISN radio is today," I said when everyone had left.

"Sure thing, Billie." Martin turned on the radio and the announcer said, "Please send, And now..., eek, eek, 'Purple Haze.'"

"Oh, there, there it is, Martin. Jimi. You got him. Turn it up!" I said as he found our home of rock 'n' roll.

> *"Purple Haze all in my brain, lately things don't*
> *seem the same, actin' funny but I don't know why,*
> *'scuse me while I kiss the sky."*

Martin and I both sang along when Jimi got to the "'*scuse me while I kiss the sky*" part.

The only nurse who didn't go outside was still at her station, behind the glass doors just outside the ward. She must have heard our loud music, but she just smiled and read her newspaper while we sang along.

There were two or three other new patients who heard Martin and me and decided to join us, sending us into full-on party mode. Martin was the only one who couldn't get out of bed, but he became a conductor, waving his hands back and forth.

The Temptations:

"So get ready, so get ready 'cause here I come,
I'm on my way (Get ready 'cause here I come)—on my way!"

Nancy Sinatra:

"These boots are made for walking, and that's just what
they'll do. One of these days these boots are gonna walk all
over you. Ready boots? Start walking!"

And with this one, I did some exaggerated walking.

When the Beatles came on, nothing could hold me back. I took my toothbrush in my hand and pretended it was a microphone, jumped up on my bed, and sang, *"She loves you, yeah, yeah, yeah, she loves you, yeah, yeah, yeah, she loves you, yeah, yeah, yeah, yeah, yeah,"* shaking my short mop like the Beatles did. My friends sang and danced right along with me, even though some could barely move. For patients like Martin and me, this was the best therapy we could ask for. Martin was blissed out, as he always was when he heard music. Afterward, when the other patients were about to return to their rooms, I looked out at our friendly nurse. Her smile was much brighter.

Those looking in from the outside might have simply seen our medical conditions—and yes, there were many sad maladies, to be sure—and felt sorry for us. But for many of us, for the first time in our lives, we were in a structured environment where we could depend on three healthy meals every day and we were even served snacks in the evenings. Plus, *our favorite TV shows* on color TV and all the rock 'n' roll anyone could want? I was sad when I had to leave. But after two months, my arm was made whole again, and I was able to return home. The inability to take P.E. or participate in rough sports as a child, didn't bother me in the slightest—I'd never liked sports anyway.

CHAPTER FOUR

While I was in the hospital, my mother met and married a Hell's Angel, and moved our family out to Newport, Oregon, about two hours south of Portland, to be with him. At that time, my half-brother Corey, lived with his father in Portland and my older brother Steve had been sent to live with his grandmother Casey, when I was five. It was now just my younger brother Bret, my older sister Valerie and my Grandma Grace. When I met my mom's new husband, I was surprised to see that he was a soft-spoken man and looked like James Dean. He played in her band while she sang.

I started fifth grade with no friends and no desire to make any. After a couple of weeks, though, a cute dark-haired boy named Paul asked me to hang out at his house after school. I realized he was a Bible-thumper when he began singing, *"It's the B-I-B-L-E, yes that's the book for me!"* on the way to his house. We hiked through a small, forested area with lush, green overgrowth and an occasional sand dune to get there. I was amazed to see that his house sat on the edge of a huge cliff overlooking a vast area of sand dunes.

When we went inside and I saw that his mother had just stepped out of the shower and was wrapped in a towel. She stood over an ironing board holding the towel with one hand and ironing with the other. When Paul left the room, she lost her concentration and dropped her towel; I quickly looked away, pretending I didn't see her naked butt. She turned to see if I was watching while snatching up the towel again. She reminded me of the centerfold in a *Playboy* I had recently pulled from a waste bin behind the local supermarket. The only thing missing, was the wink.

On the way home from school, Paul and I had discovered that we both liked to fish; however, I didn't have a fishing pole.

When Paul came back into the room, unaware of what had happened in his absence, he introduced me to his mother.

"Hey, Mom, this is Billie. He's a new kid at school and lives just across the dunes. He needs a fishing pole and wants to sell some blackberries."

"Oh, oh, of course, honey. I'll pay twenty-five cents a quart, and I'll buy as much as you two can pick," his mother said.

I couldn't help but wonder if she was being generous out of embarrassment or if she really was that nice all the time. But it didn't matter—I now had the means to buy a new fishing pole. As for the berries, we were in luck there too. There were miles of blackberry bushes in Newport, and they were just becoming ripe. After two weekends of picking, I made the $2.50 I needed for my fishing pole. It even came with a spinning reel, and I couldn't wait to get down to the docks and try it out.

It was a chilly Saturday morning, with the sun just coming up when Paul and I hiked down to the docks. Paul gave me some of his extra fishing line, and I found all the hooks I needed snagged on the edge of the dock, left by fishermen who couldn't be bothered to retrieve them. As the fishing boats came in, I asked the fishermen for the guts they didn't need. Fish guts worked well as bait.

I was ready to cast my new fancy pole out into the Newport Bay. "Okay, Paul, watch this. See that piece of seaweed out there?"

With careful aim and a gentle grip, I put my fishing pole behind my head and tried to cast the line, sending my bait toward my target. That's how it was supposed to happen. But my gentle grip was a bit too gentle, and I watched with horror as my new rod and reel flew out of my hands and into Newport Bay. For a split second I was tempted to jump in after it.

"Oh my God, Billie! What are you going to do now?" Paul asked.

Although he and I went home empty-handed that day, my desire to catch fish didn't wane. A few days later, I asked my grandma if she would like go fishing with me. Puzzled, she asked, "Billie, you lost your pole. How are you going to fish?"

"I'm making my own pole, Grandma," I told her. "I'm going to cut a straight branch from the big bushes in our front yard, and I can find everything else on the dock."

She looked a little skeptical, but agreed to join me on my Huckleberry Finn adventure the following morning. The docks floated on the water, and there were long, sloping ramps for access from the sidewalk. Grandma remained on the sidewalk and watched as I went down to the water. Like last time, I found hooks snagged on the sides of the docks, and this time I even found a wad of fishing line still attached to one. A fishing boat came in, and they were happy to give me their scraps. I was ready.

I tied the fishing line to one end of my stick, put a small piece of fish gut on the hook that was already there, dropped it in the water, and waited. It was only a few minutes before the tip of my pole began pulling wildly. I snapped it up and pulled in a large ocean perch.

"Grandma, Grandma. Look! I got one," I yelled. I didn't have an icebox or any way to store my fish, so I laid down my pole, retrieved the hook from my fish's mouth, and took it to Grandma to hold for me. She put my catch in a bag she'd brought, and I walked back to try my luck again.

I baited up again and dropped my line in the same spot as before, and this time, boom! I had a strike as soon as the bait hit the water. It was another beautiful ocean perch. I looked up at Grandma with a huge smile and proudly marched my catch up to her.

That scenario repeated three more times, and after I caught number five, I figured I would call it a day. I'd just caught five beautiful ocean perch with a twig in less than an hour. When I went back to Grandma with my last fish, she was beaming.

It was only Val, Bret, Grandma Grace, and I at dinner that evening. As we ate the fish dinner Grandma had prepared, she said, "Billie caught these lovely ocean perch this morning off the docks using only a stick for a pole! And you should have seen the pesky tourists. By the time Billie had number five hooked, they were right on top of him! But it didn't do them any good. Not even with their fancy poles and equipment. They couldn't catch a thing, but Billie was catching one right after another!"

Grandma Grace's proud smile caused my heart to swell like never before. And though Valerie and Bret didn't say much, they did seem to enjoy that dinner a bit more than usual.

The following Monday after school, I asked Paul if he wanted to hang out at my house for a while. Now that Paul and I were close friends, I felt I could confide some of my more personal thoughts. We began walking behind the Safeway store when I spotted something familiar. A *Playboy* magazine. *Oh boy!* I thought. I'd found one of these here before.

"Ooh la la. Check it out, Paul! Miss January," I said, holding up a weathered copy of *Playboy* magazine.

"Let me see. Let me see!" he said as he scrambled, trying to find the centerfold nude picture. "Woo-hoo. Check her out, Billie."

"Oh, man!" I said.

We decided to take a little break and sat there for the next thirty minutes, admiring the girls of *Playboy.* On the way home from school the next day, I decided to take a shortcut thought the woods so I could talk privately with Paul.

"Hey Paul. Have you ever played nasty?"

"Nasty? What do you mean?"

"I mean things like putting on women's underwear."

"No." He laughed.

"Do you want to try?"

"Oh, I don't know. Maybe," he said.

Maybe? I thought. His lukewarm response made me feel awkward, but because it wasn't an outright rejection, I stuck to my plan.

When we got to my house, Grandma was the only one home, and she was taking a nap. I quietly went into my mother's bedroom and found a couple of girdles, which I hid under my shirt. I went back outside and looked for a place we could try them on.

"Hey Paul, let's go over there. Those two big bushes are perfect," I said.

Once we were hidden, I handed Paul a girdle, pulled my pants off, and slid one on myself. Although it felt a bit snug, I loved it. It made me feel warm and soft inside.

"Paul. Got yours on?" The bushes were dense, and once in, we couldn't see each other.

"I don't know, Billie. I don't think I want to," he said.

"Oh, well. No problem, Paul," I said. And I put my pants back on and got the girdles back into Mom's room before Grandma woke up.

I was so hoping that in Paul I'd found someone like me, someone to validate my curiosities. Instead, I was left feeling silly and full of shame—like an oddball, a freak. I never talked to Paul about it again.

One afternoon when I got home from school, my mom and her husband, JC, were there. That was a rare occurrence, but I was determined to make the best of it when I saw what

JC was driving. Instead of his huge hog, he had a small Vespa motorcycle and was sitting on it smiling when I walked into the backyard.

"Hey, Billie. C'mere! Hop on," he said, pointing to the seat behind him. When I climbed up onto the seat, JC flew out onto the sand dunes that made up our backyard. I had to grab his waist to keep from falling off. We flew up one dune just to turn around and create another dust storm coming down. Up and over, over and across, back and forth we flew. After about twenty minutes, we were both crusted with sand and went in to wash up. At that point, he totally had my heart.

Once we got cleaned up, I went into my bedroom to do some homework. I stepped into the kitchen for a glass of water and saw what looked like a problem brewing in the living room between JC and Mom. I stepped back so they couldn't see me and watched.

JC had a letter in his hand and stood next to Mom with his right foot on the coffee table, reading it.

"Jay! Give it back. I swear—it's nothing! Please, Jay. Please," Mom cried.

JC took his foot off the coffee table and, still reading the letter, walked quietly toward their bedroom. My mother became hysterical, screaming, "Please don't go. It didn't mean a thing. I'm sorry. It didn't mean a thing."

Without a word, JC packed a bag, went outside, and tied it to his hog. Mom grabbed the coffee table and smashed it to pieces against the wood floor. I had never seen her act so violently. I crept back to my bedroom, crawled into my closet, and wept.

JC started his bike and drove off. He just drove away, and I never saw him again.

CHAPTER FIVE

After Mom and JC split up, we returned to Portland. I decided I was going to make the best of things as I began in a new school. It was the summer of 1965, and the music was incredible. I made a new friend and eventually was again flying high and free. Mom had to go on the road again, so Grandma Grace was still taking care of us. School was out, and summer vacation was well underway.

It was a warm summer evening when I went to sleep to the sounds of "Turn! Turn! Turn!" by the Byrds playing on the small transistor radio on my dresser. I was exhausted from the neighborhood explorations I'd been on with my good friend Mike and forgot we had further plans for that evening.

Our new home was in an old, single-story fourplex, located in the poorest part of Southeast Portland, and I was sleeping next to a half-open window trying to catch some of the cool evening air. All of a sudden, I was awakened by Mike's voice saying, "Billie, Billie, wake up. C'mon, it's time to go!"

Mike and I had picked up some bad habits that summer. One of them was jockey-boxing cars. We snuck out late at night, slipped into unlocked cars, and stole anything we could get our hands on—can openers, cameras, small change, and whatever was in the car's glove compartment, or jockey box.

"Where are we going?" I asked.

"Across from the 82nd Street Drive-In. We're going to make a real haul tonight."

I quietly slipped out the bedroom window, and we patrolled our neighborhood, smoking cigarettes that we found in a car. We checked every car we passed, searching for the jackpot. It was amazing how many cars were unlocked, even in that poorest of poor neighborhoods.

"Mike, check it out," I said, holding out the treasure I had just taken from a pink Lincoln Continental. There was enough change to keep us both fed at McDonald's for a week, several pieces of costume jewelry, and, much to Mike's surprise, some colorful women's panties. I put them on the bottom of my pile and hoped he wouldn't see them.

No such luck. "Shit, Billie!" he said. "What's up with the panties?"

"Oh I just grabbed everything I saw. I'm going to give them to my sister," I said and went back home.

I certainly wasn't going to tell him I'd snagged them for myself. By then I had collected at least one girdle, a couple of bras, and several pairs of panties I tried on occasionally after everyone was asleep. I felt so comfortable in them, and the silky softness of the material against my skin was heavenly.

I had a huge pile of everything we collected that summer, right there in the middle of my bedroom floor.

"Where did you get these things, Billie?" asked my grandma.

"Oh, I found them," I said. Now, if Grandma was at all suspicious, she sure waited a long time to tell me. That was the day I got busted.

During one of our jockey-boxing excursions, I had come across a small .25-caliber pistol. Of course, I thought it was the coolest thing I'd ever seen, and I often carried it with me when visiting Mike at his house. Another friend of ours, Brad, was there one day when I foolishly started showing it off, waving it around and trying to be cool. This was not a smart move at all. Brad, it seemed, couldn't wait to get home and tell his mother. The next thing I knew, there was a police officer knocking at our front door.

"Ma'am, I have reason to believe that there's a stolen gun here in the hands of a young boy named Billie. May I come in and look around?" he asked when my grandmother opened the door.

Grandma glanced at me, and the officer did too. "Okay, Billie," he asked, "where's the gun?"

I ran over to Grandma and looked up at the police officer, fighting back tears.

"C'mon, Billie. Where's the gun?" asked the officer again.

"Oh, all right, I'll get it."

"No," he snapped. "Just point to it." So I directed him to my private stash, where he retrieved the gun. He came out of my bedroom with a stern look on his face and told me to follow him back to the living room.

"Sit down, Billie. We need to talk. You're in a lot of trouble. Do you understand that?" he asked.

"Yes," I said, tears flowing.

"Do you know I could take you to jail for this?"

"Yes," I said.

"But I tell you what. I can see that you're probably a big help to your grandmother and putting you in jail would make it hard for her. I'm going to put you on house arrest. That means you won't be able to leave your house without an adult until school starts again. Are you willing to follow these restrictions and stay out of jail?"

"Oh yes. Yes!" I said, wiping my cheeks.

"Well, all right then. I'm going to patrol your house every day, and if I catch you wandering away, you know where I'll take you—right?"

"I won't go anywhere. I promise!" I said.

I was lucky that I had never been in trouble before and, of course, because I was only ten years old, they were light on me. And though it killed me to be restricted to the house and not be able to go out and enjoy the sunshine, I still had a collection of girls' undies and my transistor radio.

My mom returned from her road trip just after my house arrest ended and was understandably concerned. The first thing she did was ask my older sister Valerie to keep a close eye on me.

"Hey, Mom. My friend and are going out tonight to see a movie. Can I have some money?" asked Valerie.

"Only if you take Billie with you," said mom.

"Aw, Mom. My friends are going to be there."

"Do want some money or not?"

"Oh, all right," Val said.

The movie, *That Darn Cat* with Hayley Mills and Dean Jones, had just hit the movie theaters. I was then eleven and my sister Valerie was fourteen, and she was on a mission to look good.

She and her girlfriend were going to take me to see *That Darn Cat*, but first she had to get ready. I sat outside the small bathroom mesmerized as I watched her and her girlfriend meticulously apply their makeup. They looked like fashion models. Val wore a pair of black go-go boots that went almost up to the hem of her mini-skirt. They both were excited as they checked themselves out in the mirror. The longer I continued to watch, the more my fascination increased.

"Okay. Let's go. We're going to meet some friends when we get there and have to leave you for a while," said Val.

"You're not going to see the movie?" I asked.

"Oh, we'll watch it. We just have to sit somewhere else," she said.

The theatre was within walking distance, and it was dark when we got there. The 1950s sign that hung on the movie house was lit with incandescent light bulbs and looked romantic against the twilight sky. Foster Road was a busy street, so we were careful when were ready to cross it to our destination.

"Okay, Billie. Let's go. Look both ways," said Val.

We ran across the street to the theater. There were two young men smoking cigarettes, who looked much older than my sister, out front waiting for us. They purchased tickets for all of us, and we entered the large theater.

"Okay, Billie. Here's your ticket stub. Go in and find a seat. After the movie, meet us back out here. Okay?" Val asked as she began to walk away with her date.

"Sure. No problem," I said after taking a smoke from her. And there she was, just like my mom. Getting all kinds of love and attention after making herself beautiful. I went in and enjoyed the movie.

CHAPTER SIX

Over the next two years, we moved three more times, all still in Portland, as my mother's singing career began to slow down. I had just turned thirteen and my mother needed a place for us to stay until she could find another job. One of her girlfriends, Alice, invited the four of us to stay with her until she could get back on her feet. Grandma Grace moved back to her hometown of Junction City, Oregon; Mom and Val shared a guest room; and Bret and I slept on the living-room floor. The apartment was a small two-bedroom, barely large enough for a young couple just starting out, let alone five people.

"Okay, Billie, you need to be up and ready to go by seven-thirty tomorrow. I need to get back here by nine to get Bret to his class. Val's going to take the bus, so she's on her own," said mom.

"Ha! I do what I want, when I want, by myself now, Billie. Mom doesn't trust you," Val said after Mom left the room. At sixteen, Valerie pretty much had a free ticket to come and go as she pleased. But if Mom saw half of what I saw! The older, sex-crazed boys, the pot and booze. In exchange for my silence, I was allowed an occasional cigarette and drink.

I was in the seventh grade and very sensitive about who I was around. So when Mom introduced me to Woodstock Elementary School, I was scared to death. Most of the boys were bigger than me, and my first exchange was with the school bully, Bruce, who had a special welcome for me. When the last bell rang and I walked down the hall, several students stared at me. As the stares became glares, I looked down at the floor and walked faster. Then my books went flying out of my arms.

"Hey, Billie. I think you're a wuss!" yelled Bruce, pushing me to the ground. By then, other kids had circled us, and Bruce was their champion. They began chanting, "Bruce, Bruce, Bruce!" as a couple boys spat on me.

Bruce had his fists in the air. "C'mon, pussy. Show us what kind of a man you are. Fight. C'mon, throw a punch."

"Bruce, Bruce, Bruce, Bruce," the other kids kept chanting.

I began to cry as Bruce hit me, causing the crowed to laugh and cheer harder. Fortunately, a teacher came running to break things up. Everyone scattered except me.

"Are you all right?" asked the teacher.

"Yes. Yes, I'll be fine," I said with a sniffle. And I turned and went home. I felt so sad and humiliated. I became paranoid going to and from school after that and chose side streets less traveled, to avoid others.

After a week there, I had zero hope of making friends. As I was walking home one Friday, I looked up into the cloudless sky and lit up a cigarette. I began to blow some smoke rings when I heard someone behind me.

"Hey. Hey, man. Wait up!" a red-haired boy yelled. "Can I bum a smoke?"

"Sure," I said, handing him a Camel Light.

"I'm Randy," he said.

"I'm Bill Casey."

"I know. I'm in your class. I sit in the back, and I heard the teacher introduce you. By the way, Bruce is an asshole. I heard what he did to you last week. Someday he'll get his. Just stay away from him and his friends and you'll be fine. The only reason I come to this school at all is because my mom said she'd call the cops if I didn't. But I don't spend a second more than I need to here. Hey, man, I'm going to call you Casey. Is that all right?"

"No problem. A lot people call me by my last name," I said.

"I'm having a party tonight. Wanna come?"

"Sure," I said.

"There's going to be drugs and booze. Is that a problem?"

"Oh, no problem at all."

"Far out, man! Here's the address. Bring money. You gotta buy your own drugs." He handed me a slip of paper.

Mom wasn't home, so I left a note saying I would be out late.

I thumbed a ride to the party and got dropped off two blocks from the address Randy gave me. It was an older house with a basement, and as I approached the front door, I heard "Magic Carpet Ride" by Steppenwolf blasting from a stereo. The basement windows were all illuminated with alternating red, blue, green, and purple lights. I knocked on the door, and Randy opened it with eyes as bright as oranges.

"Casey! All right, man. Hey, everybody, this is Casey. Come on in, man. Just be casual. Dig the sound, check out the chicks, and don't worry about the drugs. Everything here is safe and pure. Party time, man. Have fun!"

I was immediately taken in by the sweet sound system, and after ten minutes, a cute girl approached me.

"Hi, Casey. I'm Linda. Wanna party with me?"

"Sure," I said.

"Have you ever done Purple Haze?"

"No," I said.

"Oh, it's wonderful. It's only five dollars. Just put it under your tongue and let it dissolve. I took mine a half hour ago and I'm really digging it."

"Okay," I said and handed her a five-dollar bill.

For the first time in my life, I had a girl on my arm while I was high on LSD, partying like a playboy. As the night went on, the music and the colors became more spectacular and I lost my sense of time.

"Linda, are you hearing what I'm hearing?" I asked and began to laugh.

Linda began laughing too and said, "No, man. What are you hearing exactly?"

The whole room began to pulsate. The laughter and the music began to echo and become hard to understand.

"Everything's getting crazy echoey. You can't hear it?"

"Oh yeah, now that you mention it, I do. And check out those color streams. Whoosh, whoosh, whoosh. This is some crazy shit!"

I began to look for a place away from the crowd to crash with Linda, and I saw three doors at the other end of the basement. I opened the first, and no one was there.

"Hey, Linda, look what I found. I think we better duck out and be alone for a while. There's no one in here."

"Oh, yeah. Far out," she replied.

The first thing I noticed as we staggered in was a mattress on the floor. We were still laughing and found it very hard to maneuver without tripping on something, so we fell onto it.

"Hey, Casey, have you ever been in bed with a girl before?" Linda asked.

We both stopped laughing, and I was completely taken off guard, so of course, I did what any horny fourteen-year-old male would do: I lied. "Oh, sure. How about you? Have you ever been in bed with a guy before?"

"Let's just say I get around. You seem pretty nervous. Are you going to be okay if we get it on?"

"Oh, I'm fine. I'm just high."

"Cool. By the way, Casey, has anyone ever told you that you have gorgeous, feminine eyes? God, with a little makeup, you'd be prettier than me. And I love your name."

I was stunned at her comments and either too timid or high to respond.

I woke up the next morning with Linda asleep on my chest. That was a first for me, and it felt wonderful. Only a few of us had spent the night, and the others were still crashed out on the floor. Linda gave me her phone number and made me promise to call her soon. We then kissed and said our goodbyes. When I got back to the apartment, my mom still wasn't there. Val was at a friend's house, and Bret was watching Saturday-morning cartoons.

I decided to call Linda to see if she wanted to hang out. Anything was better than being in Alice's apartment.

"Hi, Linda. What are you up to? Did your parents yell at you for being out all night?" I said.

"No. They were still asleep and didn't even know I was out. How about you? Did you get in any trouble?"

"No. My mom wasn't here when I got back."

"Hey, I know you go by your last name, but I just heard a new song by the Poppy Family, 'Which Way You Goin', Billy?'" Linda said with a laugh. "Of course I thought of you. And hey, can I go too? Seriously, I love it! So cute."

"Yeah, yeah. Next you'll be telling me how much you dig 'Wedding Bell Blues' by the Fifth Dimension," I said.

"As a matter of fact…"

"Okay, okay. Hey, I think I hear my mom coming. I'll have to call you back."

I'd just met her the night before and already she was serenading me love songs. I decided to wait awhile before taking her out again.

We were barely with Alice a month before Mom found a new job and we moved into a new house. I had made enough progress at my earlier school to advance to the eighth grade and attend Jason Lee Elementary School. I was small, had long hair, and wore Beatle boots and hot, lemon-yellow bell-bottom pants with a matching, button-up, long-sleeved Nehru shirt. Most boys wore jeans and button-up, short-sleeved shirts. It seemed that I was always a target for the local bully no matter where we lived.

On the way home from school one afternoon, I saw some colorful writing pens on the ground, grabbed the pink and lavender ones, and put them in my pocket. After going a couple more blocks, I noticed two older boys who looked like high-school seniors standing with their arms crossed and their feet apart, blocking my path. They both looked like some kind of linebackers, bulky enough that they didn't need protective gear to play football.

"Hey, pretty boy. Where do you think you're going?"

The other linebacker stepped up alongside his friend and said, "Yeah, man. This sidewalk is just for guys, and I think you look like a bitch!"

I froze, petrified. One of the boys pulled the pens from my shirt pocket, looked at them with a smirk on his face, and then looked at me with a menacing smile.

"Well, look at this. What do we have here? A couple of girly pens!" he said, laughing.

Then his friend grabbed them. "Yeah. Pink and purple."

I wanted to run but couldn't move.

"Let's see how good these things write," the boy said. The other grabbed and held me while the first began writing all over me.

"Nice. They write pretty good on the face," he said.

"Do his arms," the other boy said.

By the time they were done, I had lines across my face and down my arms, hands, and even ankles. When the boy had had all his fun, he said, "What are you doing on my street with all that ink on you? Get your ass home and wash it off. Now! Run!"

Blubbering, I ran home as fast as I could and went straight down to my bedroom, where I spent the rest of the evening weeping over a selection of LPs I had put aside for moments like this. I was pleased to see I still had Simon and Garfunkel's "*Bridge over Troubled Water*" on the turntable. There was always a song to soothe the pain.

But the day came that no amount of music would save me. After my "Purple Haze" party with Linda and Randy, I'd continued to drink and do drugs. I had tried everything from speed to pot and hashish. Although Randy and I didn't hang out often, I occasionally visited the old neighborhood, especially if there was going to be a party.

My mother developed a harsh method of dealing with my rebellion: the local Juvenile Detention Home, called JDH for short. I came into the house after being out most of the night drinking and hoped that Mom would be gone or sleeping. She was awake and waiting for me. And with no more than a "get in the car," we were off. Even though the sun was out, and even though she was smoking, she kept the top of her 1963 Ford Galaxie 500 convertible up all the way. I had no idea where we were going, but being a bit tipsy, I didn't care. I leaned over against the passenger door and tried to go to sleep.

The JDH building was an older, two-story, red-brick building situated right on the main highway. There were cyclone fences around the entire compound so high that on a cloudy day, I could barely see the barbed tops.

"Okay, Bill. We're here; wake up," said Mom.

"What, what?" I said, still half drunk and very sleepy.

"C'mon. Get out of the car and follow me."

I didn't know where we were and was too tired to ask questions. I followed Mom into the building, and she rang a bell at a counter marked, "Intake." I went over to a nearby bench to lie down while Mom talked to a large man who answered her bell. That didn't last very long at all. I looked up just as Mom left the building; the man who had been talking to her was now trying to get my attention.

"Okay, Casey. Get up. Let's go. You're coming with me," he said.

"What? Who are you? What's going on? Where's Mom?"

"Sorry, kid. You're drunk, and your mom couldn't deal with it. You're gonna have to stay here for a while. So c'mon. Get up—let's go!"

Once they checked me in, I sobered up fast. Everything became very cold and serious as quickly as you could slam a door. Mom had signed me in at the intake desk and left. A man then marched me down a long corridor, passing huge, solid-steel doors lining the way. Eventually, we came to a door marked "Boys 1," which was a ward for boys between twelve and sixteen. He gave a couple of quick knocks on the door and opened it with a key.

"Yeah, Bob. What do we have here?" asked the man on the other side of the steel door.

"William Casey, fourteen. His mother brought him in, and we're holding him on protective custody. Just sign here, Mike, and I'll get out of your hair," said the intake guard.

Mike was a bronze-skinned man who was the picture of fitness, except for the cast on his forearm.

"All right, Casey, I need you to just keep walking, all the way down to the end of this hallway. Stop in front of the showers."

I continued on, and when we got to the showers, Mike yelled, "Stop, strip! Take everything off. Then put your legs apart, arms straight out, and don't say a word."

I took all my clothes off and felt I was standing as told.

"C'mon, Casey, feet apart. Spread 'em!"

I thought, *what the hell?* and stupidly said, "Hey, man, what's …," I didn't get the rest of my sentence out before he had shoved his forearm cast under my chin, snapped me completely off the ground with my bare back against the cold wall, and said, "Listen, goddammit! When I tell you to do something, you do it now! Don't you ever fucking back-talk me, boy! Got it?"

I just nodded. After being strip-searched, I showered and put on their inmate uniform. Once I had a cell, I joined the general population and went to the TV room. I met runaways, drug dealers, and even a guy there for murder.

I was in constant fear. I was always on the lookout for the other inmates, who could corner and rape you in broad daylight in certain settings. I was even fearful of staff who were supposed to protect me. One wrong word and they may just whack you across the room.

That evening, while everyone was sent to the gym for a workout, a few of us were left behind in our unlocked cells, with no supervision in sight. It seemed odd that we weren't joining the others and even stranger that there were no adults close by. Whether by design or just chance, there was a small group of angry-looking boys across the hall who weren't going to miss an easy opportunity.

"Hey, bitch! That's right. I'm talking to you, bitch, get over here!" one of them yelled. I looked straight ahead, my eyes filling with tears, praying an adult would come back soon.

"Bitch, I said, get your pretty little ass over here!"

I stepped out of my cell and looked up at the cellblock the yelling came from. I saw an older, much larger boy standing in his doorway, looking at me with a huge smile. I counted down one wall tile at a time, from the bully's eyes down to the floor. When I stepped forward, I felt like I had lead in my feet.

"That's right. Get your pretty little ass in here. You going to be my punk?" said the boy.

I remained silent.

The cell was about twelve by twelve feet, with a steel bunk bed on each wall. The large boy stood in the middle of the room. Sitting on the top bunk was another boy his size, watching everything unfold.

"Hey, girly boy. You look like a bitch. Don't you wanna be my punk? I'll protect you," he said, moving closer to me. I began to cry.

"Aw, now, look what you did," said the other boy. "You got your punk all upset before we even got started."

I knew what was about to happen and simply fell apart. Just then, I heard the loud sound from the heavy steel doors at the end of the hall open and I saw the other boys coming back.

"Oh, shit. Get back to your cell, bitch. But remember, you're my punk—your sweet little ass is mine!" said the older boy. I ran back to my cell in tears. I woke up the next morning stone sober and horrified. It turned out that my mother was using a night in JDH to teach me a lesson for coming home drunk. The same man who had checked me in the night before came in and told me my mother was out front to take me back home. But I wasn't the same. I would never be the same again.

After I was back home, I came to fear JDH, to the point of becoming physically ill anytime Mom mentioned it. Whenever she needed a hammer, she had a very effective one.

"Where do you think you're going, Billie? Out drinking with your beer-drinking friends again? You come home drunk again, you know where we're going!"

I tried hard to stay out of trouble after being released from my initiation to the hellhole of JDH.

"Hello darkness, my old friend,
I've come to talk with you again"

Later that summer, the wall phone in the kitchen rang, and it was Randy. I had no idea that my mother was on the other line, listening in.

"Hey, Casey. What's up, man? I saw you getting checked in at JDH the other night. You were probably too drunk to notice me, but I was being booked a room too," said Randy.

"Oh, man. What a hellhole! And goddamn, I don't ever want to do that again," I said, looking at Mom's poster of Tom Jones on the living-room wall.

"Hey, I'm having a party this weekend. Wanna come? There's going to be girls and beer and acid!"

"Hmm. I don't know."

"Hey, c'mon! It'll be fun!"

I was so tempted, but all I could think of were those two thugs back at JDH who would be glad to see me again if I screwed up and was sent back.

"Oh, maybe."

"Great. See ya then," he said.

When I got off the phone, Mom charged into the kitchen, with her purse in her hand, on her way out the door. "So, you guys are taking LSD? No way, Jose! When I get back, we're taking a little drive!"

I didn't say a word. The house was an older, single-story, one-thousand-square-foot, three-bedroom tract home, made out of cinder blocks with two bedrooms on the main floor and the third in the basement. I had the bedroom in the basement.

This basement was my sanctuary. Since I had discovered my wondrous sound therapy in the '60s, music had only become sweeter and more diverse. I had so many artists, so many songs, at my disposal to enjoy as the moment would dictate. And if there were ever a time that I needed deliverance, that was the day.

Simon and Garfunkel's "Sounds of Silence" was playing on the radio, and I thought it set the mood for what I needed to do. I withdrew to the basement and turned on the small light at the bottom of the stairs. I'd built a worktable behind the stairs and had a few tools hung up above it. One was a big scraper with a huge razor blade inside. I opened it and pulled out the blade.

My mother didn't have enough room for all her clothes in her bedroom, so she had stored some of them in my closet. I slashed them to shreds.

Then I calmly and quietly lay on my bed and began running the razor blade across my wrists. There was a sharp sunbeam shining through my very small window; it was just bright enough to illuminate the blood oozing onto the bed. I could feel my life fading. I began to feel so tired, peaceful, and relaxed. But just as I was about to nod off, I looked up and saw a brilliant round light of beautiful colors, accompanied by a loud buzz. It lasted only a couple of minutes and then disappeared.

After what seemed like only a few minutes, I began to get a second breath of energy. Then my mother returned with some guy I didn't recognize.

"Oh my god, Bob!" Mom yelled.

"Quick, get me some towels," he said.

Mom handed him some towels; he wrapped them around my wrists and told me we were going to the hospital. He picked me up and took me out to his car, a beautiful white Camaro. He'd just gotten me into the backseat when a police car pulled up. My mother had called them.

As the officers tried to coax me out of the car, I began crying and screaming, begging, "No, no, please don't take me back there. I can't go back there, please, no, don't take me there."

"Take you where? Nobody's going to hurt you, son. Where do you not want to go?" asked the officer.

"JDH. Please, please, please, oh please, no! Please don't take me there."

"We just want to help you. We need to get you to a hospital."

I went limp. They put me in the backseat of their patrol car and took me to the hospital, where I got stitches to control the bleeding.

After my emergency treatment, the police transported me to a psych ward, where a psychiatrist examined me to see if I was of sound mind. During two days of observations, I became close to my counselor, Mrs. Smith, who understood my fear of JDH and hypnotized me as a part of the evaluation.

Mrs. Smith looked like a sweet grade-school teacher—she was slim, with medium-length dark hair and a cute pink dress that flowed past her knees. Before she said a word, I wanted to talk to her.

As I sat on the overstuffed recliner in her office, she said, "Hello, Billie. My name is Mrs. Smith, but please call me Mary. I see some of your friends call you by your last name—Casey. What would like me to call you?"

"Oh, Casey's fine," I said.

"All right, then. Casey it is," she said, smiling. "Casey, you were brought here under some pretty serious circumstances, and we want to help you. Do you understand?"

I nodded.

"Great. I need to get to know you a little better and would like to use hypnosis. Would that be okay?"

"Sure," I said.

"Well, fine, then. I'm going to ask you to just relax, look at this light, and silently count backwards from one hundred. And when we're done, you'll hear me say, 'You're awake now.' Understand?"

"Sure."

I looked straight ahead while Mrs. Smith shone a pulsating light on my forehead. When she said I was awake, I felt bright and awake, comforted by her gentle smile. I felt that she was my confidant and would do everything to prevent me from going back to JDH. After my session with her, a counselor asked me to go to the waiting room until they called for me. Two hours later, I heard my name.

I went in to a large room with a long table. Seated around it were the two therapists who had worked with me, including Mrs. Smith. Her face was red and her eyes were watering.

The man at the head of the table who introduced himself as the head physician asked me to stand. "William Casey. Do you understand why you're here today?"

"Um, I was told that I needed to talk with a shrink to make sure I was of sound mind."

"Well, that's correct, and we've found that you are under stress, but are psychologically fit." With that, he got up and left the room.

When I arrived at JDH, I was in shock as they checked me into Boys 3. I had huge bandages around my wrists, and all I could do was sit and stare blankly into space. I had no music, no friends or relatives who would visit— just me, by myself, broken, scared, and numb.

Because I was a medical case, they put me in protective custody, where I had no further problems with other inmates. A month later, I was released and returned to school long enough to finish the eighth grade. I attempted high school, but after being enrolled for only two weeks, I quit. It was the same bullshit; the bullies were just older.

My mother was still away much of the time trying to find more work as a singer. But for some reason, her singing career eventually came to an end, and she had to resort to tending bar.

My grandma Grace moved back in with us to help my mother during her tough times. I was determined to stay out of JDH, and my partying and taking drugs were pretty much on hold for the next two years. I spent most of my time in my bedroom, listening to my music. There were so many memories I longed to forget. The violence, intimidation, attempted rape, all because I had a small frame and liked colorful clothes. Indeed, my downer collection of records was larger than ever.

CHAPTER SEVEN

My mom found another job, and we moved into a house at the top of Mt. Tabor so she'd be closer to work. We couldn't have picked a better place for a long-haired music buff like me. It was 636 feet above sea level and offered a beautiful view of Portland. In the center of the park was a crater with a large parking lot alongside of it. That was where the action was during the summer months.

There were rock concerts, mostly by local artists, in the parking lot on a regular basis. And because our backyard emptied into the park, I had an access that most would have died for. During one of the weekend shows, I was surprised to hear a song that was on the radio all the time: "The Letter" by the Box Tops.

"Gimme a ticket for an aeroplane,
Ain't got time to take a fast train.
Lonely days are gone,
I'm a-goin' home, my baby, just-a wrote me a letter."

The band sounded exactly like the one on the radio, and I was overjoyed that they were right there in my backyard, singing their number-one hit.

I flew out the back door and through the backyard, jumped a small fence, and followed the music. There were cars parked alongside the road as far as I could see. I saw both guys and girls in cutoffs; most of the girls wore bikini tops, and the guys wore t-shirts. Many smoked pot, and beer kegs were everywhere. I couldn't resist the temptation. I walked up to a couple of nice-looking girls smoking pot and asked, "Hey man, can I have a toke?"

"Sure," they replied, laughing. I was sixteen, out of school and girl-crazy—or, more accurately, sex-crazy. I must have been attractive in my colorful bell-bottom pants, tie-dyed t-shirt, and love beads, because I didn't seem to have any problems finding hot chicks. I partied with those two girls for most of the concert. I eventually became too high and needed to go home and sleep it off. I left without even getting their phone numbers.

To have such a posh spot on Mt. Tabor to enjoy concerts was almost too good to be true, especially for a sixteen-year-old hippie. I became so crass and bold that I would sometimes take girls into our house while my grandma was home.

"Hey, man. Right this way, Julie," I said, with a beer in one hand and my arm around my date, escorting her down to my bedroom.

"Billie! What do you think you're doing? Your mother's going to have a fit! You can't do this!" said Grandma Grace.

I just laughed and went downstairs with my date.

Of course Grandma Grace didn't approve, but I ignored her. Finally, my mother got word of my shenanigans and did something that surprised me. I guess she had finally learned that JDH was no solution, so on that day, she said, "Get out! Get your stuff and just get out; I've had it!" Fortunately, Mike, my best friend from the eighth grade, persuaded his parents to let me stay with them until I could figure out where to go. Mike had also dropped out of high school, and after a few days, we decided to join the Job Corps. There, we could learn a trade and earn a GED.

After we signed up, we had a couple of weeks before we had to report to the housing center to begin training. That seemed like a great time for a road trip. We decided we wanted to experience a little of the leftover "flower power" we heard still lingered in San Francisco. Songs like John Phillips's "San Francisco" still occasionally filled the airways.

> *"If you come to San Francisco,*
> *Be sure to wear some flowers in your hair.*
> *If you're going to San Francisco,*
> *You're going to meet some gentle people there.*
> *For those who come to San Francisco,*
> *Summertime will be a love-in there.*
> *In the streets of San Francisco,*
> *Gentle people with flowers in their hair.*

So Mike told his parents that we were going camping for a week. And given our loose supervision at that time, no one objected. We hitchhiked our way to the I-5 South freeway on-ramp and stood there with our thumbs out on the hot pavement. It didn't take long before an older Chevy van stopped and let us in. The driver, a fellow long-haired hippie with love beads around his neck, asked, "Where you two headed, man?"

"San Francisco," I said.

There was a strong smell of pot in the van, and our driver had rheumy, stoned eyes. "Cool, man," he said. "If you can pitch in for some gas, we can take you all the way there."

His offer was almost too good to be true, but there we were laid back against our backpacks in his peace mobile. We stopped at the halfway point in Ashland, Oregon, and parked in a rest area for the night. We set out again in the wee hours of the morning and arrived in San Francisco just before noon. Our host let us out in Haight-Ashbury.

Mike and I stepped out onto the sidewalk, and I looked around in wide-eyed wonder. It was all true —the flower power, the tie-dyed t-shirts, the partial nudity, and oh my god, the music! It came from speakers mounted on grocery stores, from the colorful residents' transistor radios, and even from loudspeakers across the street in the park. It was better than I could have imagined.

"I love the flower girl
Was she reality or just a dream to me?
I love the flower girl
Our love shall lead the way
To find a sunny day
I love the flower girl
Was she reality or just a dream to me?"
The Cowsills

We walked our feet sore, exploring all that the Haight-Ashbury neighborhood had to offer. In the park we noticed several girls walking around topless; many had daisies in their hair. And of course, the smell of pot was everywhere.

Toward the end of the day, we scrambled for a place to sleep. We'd left Portland with very little money and hadn't planned on using any of it for travel, but the nonstop ride in the hippie mobile in exchange for gas money was too good to pass up. The old Chevy van, however, used more gas than Mike and I could have imagined. We straggled into a small convenience store and asked the cashier if he knew of any cheap rooms in the area.

He replied in an accent hard to make out, "Oh—you mean crash pads. Sure, right over there on the bulletin board."

"Crash pads?" I said. "Oh well, I don't care what they call it as long as it's cheap."

So we scanned the board and looked at the many postings. There was just one problem: they all read, "Available for one person at a time only."

"Shit, Mike! What are we going to do?" I said.

"No big deal. We just need a place to sleep, and tomorrow morning we can meet up here again."

We took turns in the phone booth and made arrangements to be picked up right there at the store. I felt that the hosts were quite benevolent. I mean, a place to sleep and they even provided transportation? And all for free? I was surprised to see that my ride was a newer white Cadillac.

"Okay, Mike, my ride's here. I'll see you back here tomorrow morning."

Anxious now for his ride to show, Mike said, "Sure thing. See ya then."

I got in the front seat of the Caddy, looked over, and thanked the driver for picking me up. He was a long-haired, small-framed guy with a bright smile, and it looked like he was wearing mascara.

"What's your name, honey?" he asked.

His question took me off guard. I mean, I was talking to a man—right? His voice sounded male but, *honey?* And makeup? The gay culture was barely visible back home, but was, relatively speaking, normal in San Francisco.

There was a part of me that was a bit frightened. I wasn't then, nor had I ever been, attracted to another man, but this was different. He didn't seem entirely male and I did feel a small jolt of electricity and excitement.

"My name is Casey."

"My name is Andi. By the way, we're having a little party back at my pad. Up for a little fun?"

Wow. He certainly didn't waste any time, I thought. And though I was still hesitant and unsure, I figured, *What the hell? We're going home soon, and who knows, it could be fun.*

"Sure!" I replied.

We pulled up in front of an old Victorian-style, two-story house. I noticed a cool flagpole with a British flag in the front yard. There were two tall, skinny windows on each level, and the two upstairs windows were pulled all the way open. When I got out of the car, I was immediately overcome by one of my favorite Jimi Hendrix songs, "Hey Joe."

Andi got out of the car and motioned for me to follow. He hurried upstairs, where several other people met us. Although a few were engaged in deep conversation, most just sat around with their eyes closed, swaying back and forth to the music. Colorful strobe lights enveloped the room.

"Hey, everyone, this is Casey. He just got in from Oregon and is crashing here tonight," said Andi.

Everyone gave me polite smiles, and a few even raised their beer mugs in my direction. I found a seat on the couch and took in the groovy sights and sounds.

"Hey, Casey, wanna tab of mesc?" asked Andi. I had taken mescaline before, and knew that, as with LSD, things would become a little colorful. I paused briefly to look around before deciding to take one.

"Sure!" I said. I popped the tab under my tongue and allowed it to dissolve. "Purple Haze" floated through the smoky air.

The lights became brighter until all I could see was a kaleidoscope of colors emitting from everything. I fell back on the couch, tripping and digging the music.

I must have fallen asleep, as I woke up with Andi kneeling over me. Everyone else had left and it was early in the morning. Without saying a word, he opened my pants and went down on me.

I didn't know how to react. But what Andi was doing felt beautiful and nonintrusive, so I just let it be. I really wasn't in much of a position to argue, since I was by myself. Shortly after, he returned to his room and we both went back to sleep.

In the morning, we awoke to the Kinks' "Lola" playing on the radio. Perfect. Andi offered me a bowl of Jell-O for breakfast, and although he seemed to be in a good mood, he didn't talk much. As promised, our individual hosts dropped Mike and me off at the convenience store in the morning, and neither Mike nor I spoke of our crash pad experience the night before. We decided to say goodbye to Haight-Ashbury and the land of psychedelic flower power. Gone less than two days, we were already broke and ready to begin our long journey back to Portland.

We made our way back to the freeway, stuck out our thumbs, and waited patiently for a ride, singing "Hitchin' a

Ride" by Vanity Fair. That time, even though it was another beautiful sunny day, getting picked up was a different experience. We waited for hours before we got our first ride, and they weren't going very far. We got three more rides before being dumped off on the side of the road, somewhere up in the mountains. By then it was nearly dark, and there was almost no traffic. We stood out there all night, desperately hoping for a ride.

Just as the sun began to rise, a long black car that looked like a limo pulled over. But our bubble popped when the driver said, "I can only take one of you."

"Go ahead, Mike," I said.

"Are you sure, Casey?"

"It's okay. It'll be much easier to get a ride by myself," I said with a big yawn.

Mike got in the limo and they drove off, leaving me standing there in the middle of nowhere. As the sun came up a little more, I looked farther up the road and saw, there in the middle of the mountains, a little country store. And better yet, there were a couple of parked semi-trucks. I hurried on in that direction just as one of them started his engine to leave. I was desperate and waved at him to roll down his window.

His big rig must have been twenty feet off the ground, and he sat at least ten feet above me. He was a large, round, balding man who looked like he hadn't shaved for a few days. He quickly rolled down his window.

"Hi. I've been standing out here all night waiting for a ride. Can you please get me out of these mountains?" I said.

"Sure, son," he said. "Hop in."

I was so relieved when he said he was headed north and was traveling right through Portland. I quickly fell asleep, thinking about my San Francisco experience: the public nudity, the incredible music, and, of course, Andi. Was Andi a girl? He acted like one, sort of looked like one, and certainly gave sex as well as any girl I'd been with. And the scary thing was, there was a part of me that was attracted to him, but not the male persona. I didn't want to think about it, but I was attracted to the female persona, and that wasn't allowed in my world.

Back in Portland, Mike and I hung out at his house, preparing to report to the Springdale Job Corps Center. When I was younger, my grandmother told me not to wear certain colors. It was an effort to protect me from a culture that considered most of the bright colors I liked suitable only for women's clothing. But once I was on my own, I gravitated to what I found lovely as a small child: pink, purple, and other bright pastels. I didn't understand what the big deal was. I was about to find out at my new home, my dormitory in the Springdale Job Corps.

I was still sixteen, with a feminine shag haircut, wearing bright, colorful clothes as we entered the official barracks as full time residents/students. Although my haircut and clothes made me stand out, I was actually lucky that the center allowed me to be admitted looking like that. The harsher, military-type dress code had just been lifted. Before, all members were required to have very short haircuts and wore military-uniform hand-me-downs.

The skies were overcast with regular rain drizzles, which was the norm for that time of year. But it was my new home, and it was comforting to know that I wouldn't have to worry about food, housing, or clothing for a while.

On our first day, we had orientation, where everyone gathered in the gym to meet the instructors and choose our potential career paths. The girls' dorms were located in downtown Portland, and their career opportunities were typical for that era: secretarial, nursing, and clerical.

"Welcome to the Springdale Job Corp Center. We're just rolling out our 1971 curriculum, and you guys are going to have three vocations to choose from this year: auto mechanics, machinist essentials, and horticulture. All three of these courses, if taken and passed successfully, will practically guarantee you work in their respective fields. We do require that you obtain your GED along with passing one of these courses to become certified."

Auto mechanics was interesting, but it seemed a little too complicated. Plants were fascinating, but I just couldn't see myself as a horticulturist. I picked machinist.

"Okay, everyone. That's all there is for this morning. You can go back to your dorms for two hours of free time," said the administrator. Everyone slowly filed out of the gymnasium and walked toward their dorms.

"Hey, bitch!"

What in the world, I thought as I spun around to see who was saying such crap.

"My name is Fred, and I think you look like a bitch."

That was my first exchange with a fellow Job Corps student. I ignored him and kept walking toward my dorm. Although I was frightened at first, he was a lone ranger in a sea of new students, and I felt safe there. In fact, the day before, I had met an old friend of my mother's. He was a middle-aged African-American and was one of the bus drivers for the center. He came up to me waving, "Hey! Come on over here. I'd like to talk with you." I walked over to the bus to see what he wanted.

"Are you Bill Casey?" he asked.

"Yeah. But you can call me Casey," I said.

He put on a huge smile, flung his hand back, and said, "Cool. Hey, man, give me five. I'm Clay. You don't know it, but back in the day, your mother and I performed together. She was quite the singer, on her way to some great places. What's she up to these days?"

I told him that her singing career dwindled and she eventually began tending bar. He was surprised, but understood. We talked awhile longer, and I left feeling like I had at least one friend on campus.

The next day I ran into a small guy playing an electric guitar in our dorm. We had just left the mess hall from breakfast and had some free time. I sat down to enjoy his music. After a few minutes, Fred came in and wanted to play the guitar.

Right in the middle of a song, he said in a loud voice, "Hey, man, let me play that!" The little guy ignored him.

"Hey, motherfucker. I said give me the god damn guitar!"

My new friend became visibly shaken, but didn't skip a note. That was when Fred pulled a huge hook knife from his pocket, pressed the open curve of the blade against the little guy's wrist, and seethed at him. He handed over the guitar, but fortunately, he wasn't without it for long. Fred was letting everyone know early on who the boss was, but after only a couple of weeks, a Job Corps staffer caught him picking fights and sent him packing. That was one thing I really appreciated about being there. They had a professional staff that looked out for the residents.

They also cared about our emotional well-being. One weekend they treated us to some musical entertainment by a visiting superstar who would leave a lifetime impression on me. The girls were bused in for that event, and I couldn't wait to check them out.

The staff led us all into the gym and asked us to sit while we waited for our entertainment to begin. I had no idea who it was going to be. There were no chairs, so I looked around for an open space on the floor. I looked toward the back of the gym and saw a beautiful blonde girl, with just enough room next to her for me to sit. Even though I had a reputation for being girl-crazy, I was in fact shy when it came to introducing myself. But I did manage to strike up some small talk.

"Hi. I'm Bill; my friends call me Casey. Can I sit here?" I asked, pointing to the spot on the floor beside her.

"Sure," she said with a smile. After I sat down, another male student next to her looked at me with a scowl on his face and said, "You look like a bitch!"

The cute girl said to me, "Hey, it's okay if you're gay."

By then, the floor had become uncomfortable, and I found another spot to sit, by myself, across the gym. Just as I sat down, someone came to the microphone to introduce our entertainment.

I didn't realize how famous she was at that time, but I was certainly familiar with the song she sang. I heard it on the radio all the time.

"R-E-S-P-E-C-T
Find out what it means to me
R-E-S-P-E-C-T"

It would be years before I learned what an honor it was to see and hear Aretha Franklin up close and in person. I guess I was just a narrow-minded Beatle freak and her sound was a little too advanced for me. But that music wasn't the only sound I snubbed. Even some of my Grateful Dead friends referred to me as a Beatle freak. And those who weren't my friends were either calling me a bitch or a "candy-ass Beatle freak." I felt somewhat isolated at this, and built a wall between most of the world and my chosen music to protect myself.

I began studying for my GED and working on my machinist training course. It was a disciplined program, which meant there was no sleeping in. In some ways, it still resembled aspects from the military. Every dorm had a dorm leader who was responsible for getting students up in the morning and off to breakfast.

"Get off the bed! C'mon, god damn it—I said get off the bed!" yelled our dorm leader as I was still in a deep sleep.

"What's a matter, Casey? Stay out last night partying? Now c'mon. Get off the bed!" he said to me as I seemed to be one of the last stragglers that morning. And my dorm leader was a huge guy that you wouldn't want to anger. So I didn't waste any more time and got up.

There were tight schedules, strict rules, and when I wasn't studying, there was building maintenance we all took part in. For the first time in my life I was living a structured life and becoming self-disciplined. Until the weekend. Then we had free time!

Mike and I decided to have a little fun at Dabney Park, which was right next to the Job Corps center. There often were parties where people were usually passing around alcohol and pot, and there were always cute girls looking for Job Corps recruits.

"I'm ready for a hot babe and feel like getting drunk. Let's go!" said Mike. So we slipped out the back door of our dorm room and followed a well-blazed path to the park. It was just getting dark when we made it to the parking lot.

"Hey, Mike, check out that brand-new Plymouth Gold Duster! There's at least two girls in it," I said.

"Yeah, two for me. We'll need to find one for you," Mike said with a chuckle.

When we walked up to the car, we saw that the girls were clearly stoned. A short-haired redhead sat in the driver's seat, and in the passenger seat was a big-boned girl with blond hair. They were completely oblivious and had no idea they were being stared at by two wildly interested Job Corps students. I tapped on the driver's-side window.

"Hello. Hello," I said.

The redhead was startled and rolled her window down. "I'm sorry. I didn't see you."

"No problem. My name is Bill Casey, and this is my friend Mike. Can we have a toke of whatever you're smoking?"

"Oh, sure. Come on; get in. You guys can sit in the back. I'm Diane, and this is Brit." She handed me the doobie as we settled into the backseat.

"This is a very cool car, Diane. It still has the new-car smell," I said, choking a little on the pot smoke.

"Yeah, my dad won it on a radio contest. I get to drive it all the time though. We love it!"

After another hour of talking and smoking, I said, "Hey, Diane, I'm totally blistered. I need to get back to our barracks while I can still walk. Can I have your phone number?"

"Sure. Here you go." She scribbled her number on a small piece of paper.

As Mike and I staggered out of her car, I waved and yelled, "I'm going to call you. You're going to hear from me!"

We all became friends with a common goal: party hearty! For Mike and me, that meant drinking ourselves into oblivion.

And though I continued in the program and graduated in just under a year, I also became a problem drinker. I drank at least every weekend and it was never social drinking; I drank to get drunk.

It was quite an achievement to make it all the way through the Job Corps program; the dropout rate was very high. With the machinist training completed, I was told at my graduation ceremony that I should have no problem finding full-time work. But would that be enough? I was about to find out as I entered the darkness and confusion of the adult world.

Chapter Eight

I left the Job Corps at seventeen with a new set of clothes and a thousand dollars. I found a small studio apartment, bought an old 1960 Buick for fifty dollars, and set out to find a job. Most of the machine shops were located in Northwest Portland. I drove there to look for a job and saw a sign on a pole that read "Perry's Machine Shop." I pulled over and saw an elderly gentleman, limping along with a cane, coming up to my window.

"Hello there, can I help you?" he asked in a gruff voice, leaning on his cane.

"Hi. I'm Bill Casey, and I'm looking for work. I've just graduated from the Job Corps machinist training." I said.

"Do you have any experience working as a machinist?

"Well, no."

"I really need somebody with experience."

"Well, I've gotta start someplace!" I said.

He paused briefly, then smiled. He must have liked what he saw, because he said, "Okay. I'm Perry. I'm going to take a chance on you. When can you start?"

"Now!" I said.

Perry chuckled and told me to go inside and see his secretary to do the paperwork, and to come in Monday. It was a small shop with only four other machinists. I was surprised to have been hired—after all, I was so young, I had long hair, virtually no experience, and Perry's shop was the first place I applied. I had a car, a place to crash, and now, the means to support myself. What more could anyone ask for? Apparently, a lot.

My first day on the job was easy. Perry started me on a machine that seemed to agree with me, and I caught on in no time. At the end of my first week, I saw a for-rent sign only two blocks from the shop. I figured that since things were going so well with Perry, why not be closer to work? I checked it out and discovered it was a one-bedroom apartment for twenty dollars less than I was paying. Because I had so few possessions, it was an easy Saturday-morning move.

The atmosphere at the shop lightened up a bit when Perry was out. One afternoon, while working away on my lathe, a paper airplane came flying across my face, just missing my nose. The drill press operator and the three other machinists were doubled over laughing. I guessed it was some kind of initiation process, but as innocent as it probably was, I couldn't bite. I had so much pent-up loneliness and depression and just wasn't comfortable around others, especially those I didn't know. I did continue to see Diane, but it was usually just for sex.

When I got home that night, it was dark, cold, and drizzly. I went upstairs to my tiny apartment and began searching for some good downer music to enjoy with my wine. I selected "Single Pigeon" by Paul McCartney, played it loudly, and drank myself to sleep. Because I played my music loud, I always got the routine pounding on the ceiling from below, followed by, "Turn that shit down!" just as I was dozing off.

The next day when I arrived for work, the noise from the machinery was deafening, and the shop smelled like oil. Other than that, it was the same routine at work. The other machinists, Paul, Larry, and Greg, were taking a break over at Terry's drill press. Paul was a tall, slender man in his forties; Larry was a stocky man with curly hair in his late twenties; Greg, in his late 30s, was also short and stocky with a huge, curled-up mustache. Terry was a younger, dark-haired man in his twenties who always seemed to have a cigarette hanging from his lips. All four wore white t-shirts most of the time, and that amazed me. Every night I went home with soiled black clothes, but they all kept their shirts white.

At break time, I tried not to pay attention, but I couldn't help noticing that Greg was doubled over laughing with the other three. I didn't feel like taking a break and continued working until all four of them shot paper airplanes at me from different directions. Stone cold, I didn't blink; I continued looking straight ahead and working. I heard them talking in low voices.

"He's probably just a girly guy. Doesn't know how to make paper airplanes."

"Yeah."

More laughter.

I picked up my pace as I started to cry. I went home that evening and completely broke down, wondering why people acted that way. Terry, to his credit, must have felt bad for me, because he came to my apartment the following weekend out of the blue, just to say hi and to visit. He must have asked Perry for my address. I was lying on my bed listening to the Beatles LPs when I heard him knocking on my door.

"Terry! Oh, hi, man! What brings you here? Come on in," I said.

"I was in the neighborhood and just thought I'd stop in and say hi. I heard you lived close to the shop, but I didn't realize you were just two blocks away. So, whatcha been up to?"

"Not much. Just listening to my music and working. Want a beer?"

Terry stayed and we chatted for another two hours. No one had ever made such efforts to be my friend, and we were friends from then on. I don't know what he said to the other machinists, but they became much easier to work with as well. It felt great to finally be comfortable at work, but as soon as I clocked out, I felt a dark sense of gloom going back to my empty apartment.

One very lonely Friday night, I called Diane. "Wanna party at my place? It's my birthday, and I've got beer and weed."

"Sure," she said. "I'll be right over."

She still had her brand-new Gold Duster, a baby-blue fastback with black pinstripes, and I wanted to drive it. I was watching from my bedroom window for her to arrive. By the time she pulled up, I had been drinking and was already half cooked. I ran downstairs to meet her.

I opened her car door and said, "Can I take it for a drive?"

"Sure," she said, sliding across the bench seat, allowing me to take the wheel.

Diane had just graduated from high school and was living with her mother and father in Gresham, so I said, "Hey Diane, we've been seeing each other a few months now; how about I meet your mom and dad? I can drive out there right now."

"Yeah, cool! Let's go," she said.

"Hey, I'm going to stop and pick up some more beer," I said, pulling in to a small neighborhood store. Even though I was only eighteen, I had a fake ID.

I was drunk and Diane was a little tipsy by the time we got back to my apartment that afternoon. We stumbled up the stairs that led to my 1922 apartment, complete with a Hollywood bed that dropped from a wall. I opened the doors to my bed, pulled it down, and we fell on our backs, still arm-in-arm, laughing hard. We lay there talking and giggling, and all of a sudden, I got a crazy feeling within me. I got up from the bed, pulling Diane with me, looked into her eyes and said, "Diane, I want to get married. Will you marry me?"

"Oh, yes!" she said. We embraced and fell back on the bed.

I don't know if it was an act of desperation to end my loneliness or just plain ignorance, but it wasn't love. Two months later at the wedding ceremony, I had a bottle of Strawberry Hill wine hanging out of my pants pocket. But with her parents and my grandma's blessing, we were married, and we moved into a larger apartment.

After a few months, I learned about an official apprenticeship for machinists. At the time, I was simply a "machine operator," but as an apprentice, I could make a lot more money.

As a Job Corps graduate, I found it easy to get into the program, and I went to work on the swing shift at the Bingham Willamette plant, whose products were primarily valves and pumps. Working nights, in dark, industrial Northwest Portland, did little to help my feelings of sadness and depression. Between the crowded shipyards and industrial plants, there was very little room for anything else. But there was enough room for the neighborhood drinking hole, and for a regular drinker who worked the night shift, it proved to be a very handy place to stop for a beer—or two, or three. In less than a year, my drinking became a problem at home.

"Bill! Bill, why do you always stop at Jay's before coming home from work? And your drinking, what the hell? You're always drunk when you get home!" yelled Diane.

"Okay, okay, you're right. I know I drink a bit more than I should. But I just hate my job. I had no idea I wouldn't like this kind of work when I first got into it," I said. I really wasn't that good of a machinist, and I only seemed to get worse at it the longer I stayed with it. After about three years into my apprenticeship, I earned the nickname "Scrap," due to my accident-prone nature and tendency to ruin expensive naval parts, and Diane was becoming more impatient with my drinking.

CHAPTER NINE

It was 1976, the bicentennial. And of course, things weren't bad all the time. I came home after work one evening and Diane had some glorious news indeed.

"Bill, I'm pregnant!"

"What did you say?" I asked.

"You heard me. I'm pregnant."

"Wow! Fantastic. When are you due?"

"Sometime in May."

Diane and I had never discussed having children. And though I was excited, I was also in unfamiliar territory. I had no idea what to expect, what I was supposed to do, or what would happen next. But I did get a crazy zing in my heart, a feeling of happy anticipation. Something was about to happen because of me that would be precious and beautiful. I was about to be a father, and I wanted to be a good one. I made a decision then and there to quit drinking.

We were blessed with a sweet baby girl. And being the Beatle freak that I was, I encouraged Diane to name her Michelle.

From the moment we brought her home from the hospital, I sang, *"Michelle, ma belle, These are words that go together well, My Michelle."*

I loved that song, and I loved my sweet little baby more than I could have imagined.

We decided it was time to become homeowners and found a realtor who had an old, remodeled, Cape Cod house in Milwaukie, a small Portland suburb. We quickly snatched it up and began growing our family. A few short years later, January 23, 1979, Nicoleeo, or Nicole, was born.

I was still working nights as a machinist, and the pressure of raising a family, along with being married to someone by mistake, caused my depression to worsen. We fought way too much and the marriage seemed all but doomed.

I was working at a machine shop in Southeast Portland one afternoon a month after Nicole was born, when the foreman called me to the office.

"Hey, Casey. C'mon up here. There's someone here to see you," he said on the intercom.

"Are you William Casey?" asked a man I'd never seen before.

"Yes," I replied.

"I have some papers for you. Please sign here," he said.

It was the end of my shift, and I had carpooled with an older man who was waiting for me.

"Hey, Casey. Ready to go?" he asked.

"Uh, yeah. Sure," I said as I opened the envelope. After I got in his car, I pulled out the papers and read, "Petition to Dissolve Marriage." I was aghast, and my friend noticed.

"Everything okay, son?" he said.

"My wife just served me with divorce papers," I said, trying not to cry. My friend then began to tell me about the time his first marriage failed and how much it rattled his world.

He was a sweet man and did his best to console me. Even though I didn't love her, I had become used to having a family again and I just didn't see it coming. I became so distraught that I didn't even read the details in the documents nor did I show up in court. That was that, my marriage was over.

And if that wasn't bad enough, it was the late seventies, and the economy had gone straight off a cliff into a recession. I was laid off at work, interest rates skyrocketed, and it seemed like there wasn't another job to be had anywhere.

After the divorce, I decided I wanted to go to college to look into a different career path. At twenty-three, I was still young, and as it turned out, I was lucky my first wife dumped me. Although I didn't want the divorce, I did in fact deserve it. I married way too young, was drunk more often than not, and just wasn't in love.

So there I was, single again, with no job in sight. I decided to enroll at Portland State University and explore my possibilities. Mike was still in my life and was a great help during the rough times. I was always having car troubles, and I usually went to his apartment to do my repairs.

I had purchased an old 1962 Buick four-door sedan that ran well and had a straight body, but the light, metallic-blue paint job had oxidized. One weekend, when I was feeling both ambitious and bored, I headed over to Mike's to see if we could do something to cure it or at least make it look a little better.

He'd had the same problem with his old car and was able to restore it. He had found a magic buffing compound at

Shuck's Auto Parts, which was conveniently located right across the street from his apartment. Anxious to try it out for myself, I quickly ran across the street to purchase some.

"Well she was just seventeen
And you know what I mean
And the way she looked
Was way beyond compare
So how could I dance with another
Ooo, when I saw her standing there?"

It was June 22, 1979. I went into the store and found the rubbing compound Mike told me about and proceeded up to the checkout counter when—boom! I looked across the counter into two of the sweetest eyes I had ever seen. The clerk's sparkling irises temporarily short-circuited my thinking.

I was so starstruck I found it impossible to talk. I needed to escape, to get out of there before I could embarrass myself any more than I already had. I fumbled around trying to get my money out of my wallet, paid for the polish, and bolted.

No one had had that completely disabling effect on me before. I was afraid if I went back, I would be a mess and make a total fool of myself. But Mike, as any best friend would, said that I should go back and ask her out, and began prodding me to do so.

"Casey, go back over there. You know you want to. You're not married anymore, and there's no reason not to. Go ask her out or I will!"

Or I will? "*Oh crap*," I thought. He really might, and I would just die if he took her from me.

Certainly, she wasn't the first pretty face I'd come across since the divorce, but she was the only one who had ever caused me to crumble simply by looking into my eyes. And she was certainly the only one who ever rendered me deaf and dumb simply by smiling at me.

An hour later, I decided I needed another bottle of rubbing compound and went back, hoping to stay composed long enough to speak to her. And there she was, standing right in front of me with that sweet, magical smile.

I desperately wanted to ask her out, but as hard as I tried to muster the courage, I couldn't get my words to come out without tripping over my tongue. I not only chickened out that second visit, I returned two more times before I was able to garner enough confidence to say anything.

"Hi," I said. "It's too bad you have to work on a Friday night."

"Well, I don't have to work next Friday night," she said.

Looking down, I fidgeted with my hands in my pockets and asked, "Would you like to see a movie with me next week?" When she said yes, I was even more nervous.

As far as I was concerned, I had just met a real, live, supernatural being, sent straight from heaven—just for that moment, and just for me. And she had just agreed to go out on a date? A date, really? With me? For a brief second I thought I must have been dreaming, but in case I wasn't, I felt I needed to get out of there fast before she could change her mind.

I was in love, and a seven-day week all of a sudden seemed like a month. Although I was concerned about overdoing it, I called her at least once every day.

"Hello. Is Brenda there?" I asked her father the first time I called.

I heard him call, "Brenda, honey, you're wanted on the phone."

I heard what sounded like someone running down a hallway, then heard her voice saying, "Hi. This is Brenda."

"Hi, Brenda. This is Bill. I just thought I'd call and say hello. I know we're going out in five days, but anyway, how's it going?"

"I'm doing great," she said, laughing. "I've just signed up for fall classes at PSU. How about you? What are you up to? Are you in school?"

"PSU? Wow! That's amazing. I've just started there too, and yes, I've signed up for my fall classes. What a coincidence! We just met, miles from PSU, and yet, we're both freshmen there."

"I know. That is something. What classes are you taking?"

I read my list of classes and there was one that we both were signed up for—an elective, metal art.

"Wow. You're signed up for metal art too?"

"Yeah. I figured that since I was a machinist, it would be an easy credit. Plus, who knows, I may even like it," I said, and we both laughed.

We talked for at least another hour, and yet it only seemed like a few moments.

I was no longer nervous about talking with her, and as it turned out, she liked talking to me too. During our phone conversations, I learned that she was only seventeen. I was a little concerned, because I'd be meeting her parents when I picked her up for our date and I was twenty-three.

When Friday night finally came, her dad met me at the front door. He had a full beard and a smile like Brenda's.

"Hi. Bill? It is Bill, right?" he said.

"Yes, it is, but my friends all call me Casey."

"Hello, Casey. My name is Ron. I'm Brenda's dad. She'll be out in a minute. This is my wife, Beverly," he said, shaking my hand.

"Hi. I'm happy to meet you. Go ahead and have a seat, Casey," said Beverly.

I told them that we were going to have dinner at the Benihana Restaurant downtown and then see a movie. I assured them that I would have her home at a decent hour; Brenda grabbed her purse, and we left.

On the way to the car, I asked her, "So what are we going to see?"

"Oh, it's a comedy. *Apocalypse Now*," she said.

In the theatre watching the movie, I wondered, *comedy?* A blood-and-guts war movie? Later, after the show, she told me that one of her college instructors had told her it was a comedy, and laughed all the way back to her parents' house, about her instructor's sick sense of humor.

We parked, and I went around and opened the car door for my Brenda Sweet. I walked her to the door, where our eyes met for only a few seconds, but I felt that I was going to be with her forever. I leaned in and gently kissed her, and the kissing grew more passionate. Reluctantly, we pulled apart, looking at each other with eyes that wanted more.

We saw more of each other once school started. One weekend, Brenda and I were hanging out at my apartment listening to music when Mike showed up at my door.

"Casey, my car broke down and I need a jump. Can you help me out here?"

I looked over at Brenda, uncertain, but she said, "Oh, go ahead! I'll be just fine until you get back."

I drove Mike out to his car, and after over an hour of attempting to get it started, it finally kicked in and began to run smoothly. Mike took off, and I was anxious to get back to my Brenda Sweet. Once I walked in, I couldn't believe what she had done.

Brenda had washed the dirty dishes scattered everywhere and put them away neatly in the cupboards. She had completely cleaned up my messy kitchen. I was even more convinced that she was my once-in-a-lifetime kind of girl.

After an hour of talking and laughing on my couch, she suddenly gave me an incredibly serious "I want you" look. The talking was over. I took her into my arms and carried her into my bedroom, where I gently laid her on my bed. She looked at me with her dreamy eyes, our lips came together, and there was no doubt about it: I was in love.

It didn't take us long to discover that we were made for each other and needed to be together always. Brenda agreed to move in with me. I was about as poor as could be and had put an ad in the local newspaper that read, "Handyman will provide remodel work in exchange for rent." A middle-aged woman with a young daughter responded that she had a basement and wanted it converted into living space. So we created an agreement stipulating that I would build her a basement apartment in exchange for two years of rent.

Once Brenda moved in, she put up sheets for privacy and hung our clothes along the concrete walls. She was totally adapted to roughing it while I built the apartment, which caused me to love her even more.

Sex became wilder as the weeks went on. At every opportunity, we behaved like lonely, sex-deprived bunny rabbits. That was also when my feminine side began to resurface.

"Brenda, I think I'd like to try something a little different. This is going to sound crazy, but I feel a little girly sometimes," I said.

"What do you mean, girly?" Brenda said.

"Sometimes when I'm real horny, I imagine myself with women's makeup on. Playing a very feminine role while having sex. Weird, huh?"

"Oh, I don't know. I think you'd be pretty cute," she said.

"I know. It's funny. But the feeling gets so strong."

"If that's something you want to try," Brenda said, "why not?"

"Really? You'd help?"

"Sure. I like being adventurous. Come over here and sit. I'm going to put a little mascara on your eyelashes, some eye shadow and lipstick. You'll be gorgeous!" she said.

So my Brenda Sweet took her time and made me up to look as pretty and sweet as any girl on campus. And it was good, from the mascara that brought life to my eyelashes to the soft pink lipstick that made my lips look edible. But after we were done, I felt ridiculous and full of guilt and shame.

"Brenda, I don't know what's wrong with me, why I wanted to go into a girly mode and do those things. I feel so stupid and silly," I said at the kitchen sink, rinsing off my makeup as quickly as I could.

"Hey, no problem, honey. And really, what's wrong experimenting occasionally?" she said.

Because I was in the arms of someone who brought me such joy and security, I began to feel more in touch with my inner feelings of femininity—something I had been repressing for a very long time.

CHAPTER TEN

Back when I was a machinist apprentice at Bingham Willamette, I met a man who was always trying to get me into a Bible study. One of the jobs I did was working in the tool crib checking out tools to the machinists during the swing shift, so I was able to play my radio a little louder than usual.

One evening I saw a large man leaning into my service window, trying to get my attention. "Hey, ya want to turn that thing down a little? I need to check out some Allen wrenches."

I turned my radio down enough to hear him talk. "Sure. Coming right out."

"Say, I can't believe we have an apprentice I haven't met. My name is Mel," he said.

"Oh. Cool. I'm Casey."

"Good to meet you, Casey. Hey, at lunch, I'm having a little Bible study over at my machine with a couple other guys. You're welcome to join us if you want."

"No thanks," I said with a soft laugh, and walked away. It seemed that there was always somebody trying to push a Bible pamphlet into my hand. I must have been a bit rough around the edges.

After being called "scrap" too many times, I left Bingham Willamette and went from shop to shop, never staying very long at any of them. It soon became clear that I wasn't a good machinist at all, but I tried to stay with it for as long as possible for the money.

Then the most remarkable thing happened: Mel secured a job at the new shop I was at. Each time I moved to another shop—and I moved to four in less than a year—he ultimately showed up there too. And at each new shop, he invited me to his Bible study.

I eventually gave in and decided to give his study a listen, if my Brenda Sweet was willing. Brenda agreed, and we went to their home for a spaghetti dinner and the slideshow on "what it takes to become a Christian."

I went to the front door and a short, round, and very jolly woman greeted us. "Well, hello there! Come in, you guys. I'm Jan. If the dinner causes any problems, you have me to blame!"

We all dug right into the hearty pasta feast, and Jan kept the mood festive. After dinner, we moved into the living room, where Mel delivered his Jewell Miller film presentation, a well-known film series in that denomination. The last slide made it clear that if you wanted to become a Christian, full-immersion water baptism was necessary. It sounded reasonable to Brenda and me. I had been to a compelling seminar called "Evidence that Demands a Verdict" by Josh McDowell a month earlier, so I was an easy sell on the Bible, and the Bible spelled it out pretty clearly. Mel couldn't wait to get us under the liquid to be officially baptized. They drove us out to the Gresham Fourth Street Church of Christ for the baptism that same night.

Once we were authentic Christians, Mel and Jan convinced us we needed to be married in order to continue living together. But we didn't set a date immediately.

A couple of weeks later, we were having dinner at our favorite Chinese restaurant, The New Cathay. "Hey, honey. How's the chow mein?" I asked.

"Good," she said. "I love the pan-fried noodles on the side. Much better than the greasy, crunchy ones. By the way, when you going to marry me?"

It took me completely by surprise. Society dictated that men were supposed to propose to women, but I just said, "Whoa! That's right. I guess we'd better come up with a date. By the way, has anyone ever told you that you're gorgeous when you propose to them?"

We chose July 18, 1980, as our wedding day.

Brenda knew that I had two young daughters from my previous marriage and accepted them without hesitation. I picked up Michelle and Nicole on the weekends for visitation, and Brenda was a huge hit with  them from the start. She was like a second mother, doing everything from reading them stories to helping them with their "owies" from playing too hard.

I was taking tae kwon do and spent a lot of time working out at a local high school, running around their track. After Brenda and I picked up the girls one weekend, I decided to stop for a quick lap, and three-and-a-half-year-old Michelle insisted on joining me.

"I can run, I can run," she said as I stretched.

"Go ahead, honey," said Brenda, holding baby Nicole. "If she wants to run, let her. I'll follow close behind with Nicole."

So I took off, and to my utter amazement, as I rounded the track at the halfway point, there was my little Michelle, running toward me with a beet-red face. I was stunned. I couldn't believe a child so young, so little, could run like that. I picked her up and kissed her all the way back to the car.

A month before Brenda and I were married, I arrived at Diane's to pick up my girls for our weekend visit. I knocked and was taken aback when she answered the door naked.

"Hi. C'mon in. The girls are still sleeping," she said.

"Hey, I'm sorry, but I've moved on. I've found somebody else. I can wait. Can you get them ready, please?" I said.

She grabbed a robe to cover herself and snapped, "Wait here. I'll get them."

A few minutes later, my sleepy little girls emerged and were ready for the weekend.

"Daddy, Daddy," Michelle said and crawled into my arms.

"Hi, sleepyhead," I said, putting her back down so I could carry Nicole.

"I expect them back here Sunday, no later than five," Diane said.

"See ya then," I replied, and left with my girls.

The next time I attempted to pick them up, Diane said they were ill and couldn't go out. The following weekend, it was the same story. After three weeks without seeing my daughters, I called Diane to ask why she was messing with my visitation schedule. "Diane, it's been three weeks since I've seen my girls. This isn't fair. What's going on?"

"I saw you touch Michelle inappropriately. I've contacted an attorney, and they say I have a right to place restrictions on your visitation now."

"I did what? What a fucking, lowdown, evil lie. This is lower than low, even for you! You know this is bullshit."

She hung up on me.

I hired an attorney and met with him two days later. He recommended I take a polygraph test right away. I took and passed one the next day, but nothing could undo the damage she had caused.

"What can I do about these molestation charges my ex has made up to screw me out of seeing my daughters?" I asked.

"I'm afraid nothing. This is a relatively new tactic being employed, primarily by bitter ex-wives, as a form of punishment. So far, it seems to be working flawlessly in their favor. The authorities can't prosecute, as there is no evidence one way or the other; all they have is hearsay. But the courts can and do place harsh—and in your case, unfair—restrictions on the accused's visitation rights. As they put it, if they're going to err, they're going to err on the side of the child. Therefore, the best you can do is get visitation on your ex-wife's terms.

And right now, it looks like she wants you to see Michelle and Nicole in her presence at her parents' house."

"You mean all it takes is an accusation by one of these wild-eyed, bitter ex-wives to screw the husband out of seeing his children? No evidence? Just bitter women making wild claims?"

"I'm afraid so. Your best hope is that she softens up down the road and reinstitutes fair visitation."

From that point on, I couldn't take the girls anywhere, and I could only visit them in the living room of my ex in-laws, with all of them watching my every move.

Brenda and I attended a church on a regular basis and brought Sunday school materials with us to share with both Michelle and Nicole. It was hard, but we did our best to not let Diane's treatment hinder what little time I was allowed to have with them. I loved them so much and still couldn't believe that their mother would choose the actions she did. We read Bible stories, sang Bible songs, and had the best time we could under the circumstances. I was able to maintain a warm, close relationship with my girls, and they still loved me.

Shortly after my visitation issues began, Diane found a boyfriend, and he moved in with her. He quickly took her place as the overseer during my visitations, and the environment became more and more toxic for everyone present.

Brenda and I pulled up in front of Diane's parents' house for my Sunday visit, and I noticed a huge motorcycle in the driveway.

"Wow. Check out that hog! Well, at least her new ol' man has good taste in bikes. That's got to be a Harley. Very nice," I said.

"Whatever. I don't know about him, but I've totally figured her out. She's evil to the core! I can't believe she'd use her own daughters like this, just to get back at you," said Brenda.

"I know. It totally sucks, but there's nothing I can do. It's important we keep a happy face in front of the girls. It certainly isn't their fault their mother wants to be this way."

We then knocked on the front door.

Diane's new boyfriend, a balding man in glasses whose name turned out to be Ted, said, "C'mon in. The girls are right over there." He pointed to the couch.

"Hello, Ted. I'm Bill. By the way, nice hog. Is it a Harley?" I asked.

"I know who you are, and yes," he said.

"Hi, Daddy," said Michelle as I grabbed her up for a big hug. I sat with her on my lap, and Brenda held Nicole. After we giggled and talked about Michelle's doll for a few minutes, Brenda and I began singing some Bible songs. Ted was sitting across from me, looking me straight in the eyes, leaning in with his elbows on his knees, scrutinizing me. I did my best to make it work. After several weeks, however, I could tell that Michelle was picking up on my stress. What once was an environment filled with happiness and laughter had turned into an hour of painful tension. Even my girls had stopped laughing and didn't seem to enjoy my visits as much as they once had.

I began to fear that my sweet babies were succumbing to the poisonous environment. Diane's boyfriend became their active male parent, and because the setting was so bitter and tense, I decided to get out of the picture and allow them to complete their childhood years in something that more closely resembled a normal family. That was one of the hardest decisions I ever had to make in my life—to just walk away and never see them again, at least until they grew up.

CHAPTER ELEVEN

It had been three months since I saw Michelle and Nicole, and I was still finding it hard to stop thinking about them. Brenda and I were to be married soon and there were preparations that needed attention, but I was still dazed and my focus was blurred. Fortunately, I had help. We found that there were some sweet benefits to being members of a church family. Everyone knew Brenda and I were too poor to afford a wedding, and they came together to give us a decent ceremony.

Several women from the church got together and took care of almost everything. Brenda made her bridal veil, Brenda's aunt's mother-in-law made our wedding cake, and another church member loaned Brenda her wedding gown. After the wedding, we spent the first night of our honeymoon at the Portland Hilton Hotel, probably the most luxurious lodging in town. The next morning, we drove to the Inn at Spanish Head, a resort hotel just outside of Lincoln City, where our room had a balcony overlooking the sea.

"Hi, honey. Let's walk on the beach. It's a sunny morning, and there's hardly anyone else out yet," said Brenda.

"Whatever you say, Mrs. Casey," I replied.

"Oh my, that sounds so wonderful. I can hardly believe it. I'm really married."

"Yeah. And married to Bill Casey," I said, laughing. Then I started thinking of my girls again.

"Did I say something wrong, honey? You sure got quiet all of a sudden," said Brenda.

"Oh, it's nothing, honey. Seriously, I'm looking forward to spending the rest of my life with you. I was just thinking about Michelle and Nicole. I still can't believe I won't be able to see or visit them anymore until they're eighteen. It crushed me to have to give them up. It's only been a few months since I saw them, but it seems like so much longer."

"Oh, me too! It's amazing what hate can do to one's heart. But they'll grow up someday and learn the truth for themselves. And we'll eventually have a family of our own," said Brenda.

Back at our basement apartment, we received bad news from Brenda's parents. We had just begun our marriage, but her mom and dad were in the process of ending theirs. I had no idea until her dad called us to tell us he was moving into an apartment by himself. I was surprised and saddened but made it clear that nothing would change between him and me.

The basement apartment was nearing completion, and I began to think about how I was going to support Brenda and pay rent. I came up with one of the stupidest ideas of my life: I decided I wanted to join the Navy. A recruiter at PSU convinced me that if I signed up to be a Navy Seabee, I would receive all the training needed to become a plumber. I felt that I wasn't making any progress at finding a career direction at school, and Oregon's economy was in the toilet. It was 1981, and in Portland, there were no possibilities of getting into a plumbing apprenticeship in the foreseeable future.

One of the families at the church we attended graciously offered to take Brenda until my basic training was complete. I was ready to report for duty. I think I actually knew that joining the Navy was an awful decision, but I was too desperate for work to admit it.

When I'd completed all the placement testing and was about to be sworn in, it hit me: *What in the Sam Hill am I doing here?* All at once I got an overwhelming feeling of loss in my gut and almost became nauseated. But it was too late. They swore us in, transported us to the airport, and flew us straight to the San Diego Naval Base.

We arrived in the early, early morning where my nightmare went into full gear. For days I was in a state of shock, following orders, marching, and learning the game of hurry up and wait. I wanted out. I knew I'd made a terrible mistake and simply wanted to go home.

One evening, after cadence marching all day, we were given a little time in our barracks for personal activity, like writing letters to loved ones. I overheard a couple of other recruits having a conversation that pretty much summed up how I felt: the gist of it was, "What in the hell have we done?" After discussing our common stupidity, one said, "You can always tell them you're gay. They kick people out for that."

But I was a member of a very conservative church, so to claim I was gay was tough—but not so tough I couldn't pull it off. The next morning, I was mopping floors in the latrine and found myself alone with one of the training officers.

"Captain Williams, sir. Seaman Casey requests permission to speak, sir."

"At ease, Casey. What's on your mind?" he said.

"I believe I've made a terrible mistake by enlisting in the US Navy and in fact, I shouldn't be here, sir."

"What do you mean, you shouldn't be here?"

"Sir, I'm gay."

"All right, Casey. Get back to work."

And I was more or less ignored by my Captain for the first couple of days, so it was a surprise when I was transferred to a holding unit.

The holding unit was made up of recruits who were in transition or on their way out. Most were like me—confused young men who decided early on that enlisting was a mistake. But nothing happens fast in any branch of the military. It didn't matter why any of us were in the new unit; we all had a common assignment: wait. Day after long day went by with no information regarding our requests to leave. We still participated in cadence marching to and from the mess hall, but otherwise were confined to our quarters with nothing to do: no books, no electronics, just our bunks, which were separated by a long row of metal tables and benches. During the day we weren't allowed to sit on our beds, so we sat at those two cold steel tables all day.

After a week, the captain called for me. "Seaman William Casey, front and center."

I ran to the front of the room and replied, "Reporting for duty, sir!"

"At ease, Casey. I have orders to send you over to talk with Sergeant Elroy. You're to report to him at once."

The Captain handed me my orders along with a map of where to find Sergeant Elroy. The San Diego base was mammoth, and someone who was not already familiar with the layout could easily get lost. I took the map and marched what seemed like a mile and a half across the base. Sergeant Elroy's office turned out to be a small six-by-six-foot shack located at the perimeter of the base. I marched on up and knocked on the door.

"Enter!" a loud, commanding voice bellowed. "Seaman William Casey?"

"Yes, sir," I said, at attention.

"At ease, Casey. Shut the door and have a seat." The room was barely large enough for two small chairs and the small table that separated us. Sergeant Elroy was a huge man who looked like he trained bodybuilders at a gym somewhere. After I sat down, he leaned in with his nose only inches away from mine and said, "So, I hear you want to go home, to get out of this man's Navy, is that right?"

"Yes sir, it is," I replied.

"Well, Jesus Christ, kid, you just got here. Why don't you give it a chance?"

"I made a terrible mistake sir, and never should have enlisted in the first place."

"Goddammit, kid, what are you, a pussy? Why don't you act like a man? Says here you're gay. Why don't I get your wife on the phone right now and ask her about that?" he yelled.

"I don't care. As long as you don't badger her like you're badgering me," I said.

I might as well have said that I'd seen him out whoring on the boulevard, wearing a tutu.

"Goddamn, you little punk, I'm going to come across this table and smack you so hard you won't need an airplane to get you home if you talk to me like that again," he yelled. He had no plans to call Brenda once I gave him the go-ahead. He went on for another twenty minutes, trying everything he could think of to make me feel like I'd be a failure if I went through with my request. But after his outburst, I chose to remain silent.

The following morning, my captain ordered me to report to another officer. There I was treated with respect and politeness. My best guess was that higher-ranking officers had discovered how Sergeant Elroy treated me and needed to clean up his mess. Or maybe it was good cop/bad cop. But at last, someone listened to me and treated me like an adult. I received orders to go to my final unit, where I waited another two weeks before I went home. Although I felt like a complete disgrace for quitting the Navy on day one, at least I didn't get an undesirable discharge. I was issued a general discharge — neither honorable nor dishonorable.

Back at home, I found a job as an apartment manager, and Brenda and I moved right into the complex. It was very short-lived, however. The owner turned out to be a drunken ass, and neither Brenda nor I was comfortable around him. I still wanted to be a plumber, and at that point, I was desperate enough to check other parts of the country for work. It seemed like the whole world was in a deep recession.

So I made a visit to our local library to check out the help-wanted sections of newspapers around the country. In our local newspaper, *The Oregonian*, the entire help-wanted section barely took up two pages. And all the other major cities looked exactly the same, except one: *The Houston Chronicle*. When I opened its help-wanted section, I couldn't believe my eyes: it was the size of the entire Sunday *Oregonian*. Job after job was listed in the "plumbers wanted" section: "Wanted: plumber's helper." "Wanted: plumber's assistant." Every kind of entry-level position I could have hoped for was readily available in Houston.

I took down some numbers and returned home to tell Brenda. "Hey, Brenda. Check this out. There's more job opportunities in Houston than the all the rest of the country combined. What do you say? Ready for a move down south?"

"But we don't know anyone down there. And it's so far away."

"I know. And it's hot and muggy too. But I don't know where else to go. It really was the only city in the country with an abundant job supply. And besides, it will only take me four years to get my plumber's license, then we can move back."

"Oh, I know. You're right. It's just that I've never been so far away from my parents before. But I'll adjust. And, if there's that much work, I'll get a job too! So of course, darling. Go ahead and call some of those numbers and let's see what you come up with."

I got on the phone and within minutes, two different plumbing shops offered me jobs. All we needed was a truck large enough to make the move. We were in luck there too. I found somebody who swapped our older, gas-saving Volkswagen Squareback for his gas-guzzling Ford pickup; we then packed up our stuff and hit the road!

When we arrived, we found an apartment near the Bellaire neighborhood, an older residential area. Brenda got a job as a cashier at Ellen's Hallmark, and I got a job at Bellaire Plumbing as a service plumber. I had gained a lot of plumbing repair experience during my stint as a handyman in Portland, and they were happy to have me. The owner even purchased a shiny, brand-new van for me and instructed me to get it outfitted and road-ready. Back in Portland, we left dark, rainy skies and poverty, and in Texas, it was warm, sunny skies and all the work anyone could want.

One sticky, humid afternoon, we were sitting on the bed when our phone rang. Brenda's mother had remarried a police officer named Fritz, from St Helen's, just after we moved to Texas. Brenda answered the phone, and Fritz asked her to hand the phone to me. My arm felt like lead as I lifted the receiver. I knew in that split second it was bad news.

"Hi, Fritz, how are you—what's up?" I said.

"Is Brenda sitting down?" Fritz replied.

"Yes she is, Fritz. What's wrong?!"

"Brenda's dad, he's dead. He committed suicide."

I felt numb and simply hung up. Brenda and I had paid Ron a visit in his new apartment the day before we left Portland—he was such a kind, soft-spoken man, whom I had grown to love. Crying, I took Brenda into my arms and held her.

"Has something happened to Mom? What's the matter?" she pleaded.

"Your father is dead. He committed suicide," I replied. "Oh, my Brenda Sweet. I'm so sorry, honey."

And I held her and let her cry, and I cried with her. Brenda decided that returning to Portland for her dad's funeral would be too much of a hardship on her new employer, but she took a couple of days off to grieve and comfort family members over the phone.

We had barely been in Houston six months, and Brenda had already become indispensable at Ellen's Hallmark. She blossomed into leadership material, and over the next year, Ellen's Hallmark opened three additional stores. Brenda managed all four.

Brenda and I had come to love Houston and the people there, and found it to be a warm and friendly place to settle down. We eventually moved into a rental house in a newer neighborhood called Katy, just outside of Houston. It was a beautiful area with single-story houses, many with palm trees planted in the front yards and great freeway access. This was important as I had moved on from Bellaire Plumbing to another shop and enrolled into the apprenticeship.

I was still doing service calls, and after two weeks, I found myself working with an emergency crew, pulling twelve-hour shifts at the Nabisco Cookie factory. They had collapsed sewer lines inside the building, and the only way to get at them for replacement was by hand. I was one of the laborers, digging ditches over nine feet deep next to the long rows of ovens.

I was quite muscular and could jump into most ditches without the aid of a ladder. One evening while I was digging a ditch that was already three feet above my head, my boots got stuck in the Texas muck. So I took them off, threw them up out of the way, and continued to dig barefoot. Later, after a break, I jumped back in the ditch, still barefoot, just missing one of the southern laborers.

"Yayyyy....!" I yelled with my hands straight up in the air, grasping my shovel as I jumped back into the ditch.

"Damn, Bill. Where you from? You a wild man! Wild Bill. That's what we gonna to call you—Wild Bill! Yes, sir—from now on, you Wild Bill!" said the southern laborer. And from then on, they did. Apparently, some of the women who worked there must have taken a liking to me as well. After my shift was over, a couple of gorgeous southern belles gave me wolf calls all the way to my truck.

Brenda worked later hours than I did, so I often got home to an empty house. One afternoon I was scanning the local newspaper and saw an advertisement for Mary Kay makeup.

I felt a zing run down my spine when I read that I could get a free makeover in the privacy of my own home. As a new apprentice, I was spending my days in full-on guy mode, but in the quiet of my own bedroom, I found myself fantasizing about wearing Mary Kay makeup, and the thought of someone else giving me a makeover was just as exciting. I eventually called the Mary Kay sales rep to see if I could get a makeover, and she did indeed show up.

When the doorbell rang the afternoon of my appointment, a jolt of anticipation shot through my body.

"Oh, hi. C'mon in. I'm Bill Casey," I said to the Mary Kay sales rep.

She was an attractive woman in her thirties, wearing a modest tan skirt with a white blouse. Her makeup was flawless all the way down to her red lip gloss.

"Hi, I'm Kathy. Glad to meet you. Where shall we set up?"

"Oh, right over here. We can sit at the dining room table."

"All right. I must say, we don't get a lot of males calling to become sales reps. Do you have any experience with women's makeup?"

"Not really. But your ad says you offer training. That's why I called."

"No problem. So where should we begin?"

"Can you help me do up my face?"

"Absolutely! So the first thing you need to do is wash…"

For the next half hour, Kathy applied foundation, eyeliner, mascara, blush, and finally lipstick until I was transformed in to a beautiful young woman. After I applied my lipstick, she put her mirror in front of me.

"So what do you think?"

At the sight of my reflection, I felt my body go still, afraid to shatter the image in front of me. I was a twenty-four-year-old plumber, in the construction industry, down in the deep South. I was "Wild Bill." And yet, there I was in the mirror, as gorgeous as the southern belles who seemed to be so attracted to my masculine presentation. Gorgeous by anyone's standards.

"Look what you've done. I'm beautiful. There are no other words for it—I'm beautiful. Thank you." I said.

"Honey, you don't need to thank me. I think it takes real guts to do what you're doing, and I'm behind you all the way," she replied.

But my elation quickly evaporated to guilt and shame, just as it had every other time I tried wearing makeup.

After that, Kathy went over the sales plan with me and gave me instructions on becoming a Mark Kay sales rep. I thanked her for her help and quickly washed my face. After she left, I went to my bedroom and listened to my downer music. The shame I felt was overwhelming. And when I thought about how I kept my Mary Kay experience from Brenda, my sadness only increased. I was so torn and conflicted inside. I might have been a stud plumber at work, but on nights like that one, I was a beautiful girl.

CHAPTER TWELVE

We planned on purchasing our rental house once we had a decent down payment saved, but after two years, the depressed economy we left back in Oregon finally made it to Houston. All the work dried up, and there were no prospects of improvement soon. But to our good fortune, the economy in Portland started to improve in early 1983. And because I was still an a apprentice, I was in demand there.

Back in Portland, we rented an apartment, and I got a job at Oregon City Plumbing and went to work for the owner, who was also the chairman of the plumbers' apprenticeship. He was a charming older gentleman and gave me the same experience I had in Houston by treating me like a journeyman service-and-repair plumber from day one. I drove a service truck and handled repair calls from private homes.

April 1, 1984, was a golden, sunny day in Portland. I finished all my service calls and returned to the shop to drop off my truck. Just as I stepped into the store, the owner's son mentioned that my wife had called me. I knew Brenda Sweet would never call me at work unless there was a real emergency.

When I was told, "Your wife called," I knew exactly what the news was but I couldn't—wouldn't—take it in. I don't know how I knew, but I did, I knew. And I would not allow the morbid thought to fully form in my mind and become complete. Not then, no; not just like that. It could only be about Grandma Grace.

 Before I called Brenda back, my mind went into survival mode and I wandered aimlessly through the shop and picked new material for my truck. *I need material, I need material, I need to work—I will not fucking think of anything else. Oh my God. No.* I became lightheaded; my eyes welled with tears. I quietly prayed, *Oh please, please God. Please don't take her—please.*

I thought of Grandma Grace walking with me to the dock in Newport and watching me catch fish after fish. I thought of the times we had picked wild blackberries in abandoned lots. The tears flowed when I recalled the time as a very young child, when I had tried to help her in the vegetable garden, saying, "Grandma, can I help you make vegetables?"

Brenda and I made trips to Junction City as often as we could to visit her at her senior apartment center. Unlike many others her age, she spent most of her time as a volunteer, helping other seniors. And when Brenda and I had to leave, she almost always had something to send home with us.

"Here, honey," she'd say. "Take this with you. It's just a few things that wouldn't fit in the fridge." She filled her "I love you" bags with everything from blueberry cream pie to Hamburger Helper.

No, I won't call her, I kept thinking. *I've got to load my truck. I've got a lot of work to do tomorrow. I've got to work—I've got to fucking work.*

I finally realized that there was simply no escape. I went to a private phone in the back of the shop and called my

Brenda Sweet. I already knew what the news was, but still allowed her to say, "Your grandma died." She said more, but that was all I heard. It felt like my eyes were stuck, frozen wide open. Looking straight ahead, I gently hung up the phone.

Slowly and in a daze, I began my long trip home. I had a mix tape blasting away in my stereo, made up of sad songs like Aretha Franklin's "Ain't No Way." I was on the freeway and well on my way when I started thinking of the times I had been mean to my grandmother as a teenager. I fell apart while driving, crying so hard I was getting attention from other drivers. Other than Brenda, there was no one on earth I loved more than Grandma Grace. She spent her entire life doing for others. Even when they found her in her apartment, she was knitting a blanket for her preacher's newborn grandchild. Mourners packed her funeral service. Many people had been touched by her kindness.

Brenda and I continued to live in our apartment for about a year before we decided to move to a better neighborhood. We discovered a program through the State Department of Veterans Affairs that allowed people to buy houses via silent auction, and we could even use sweat equity in lieu of a cash down payment. We found a place in east Portland that needed a lot of work, but I was willing to do it to save money.

"What do you think, Brenda? Is this a place you'd like to call home?" I said.

"Absolutely, and we'll probably want to make our bid higher, considering we get the garage as well," Brenda said.

We were the high bidders, and when the paperwork was complete, we moved right in.

In 1984, I finally received my state license as a journeyman plumber and opened my own shop, Casey's Plumbing, in the garage behind the house we'd purchased. When it came to "sprucing things up a bit," I went to extremes. I had the house jacked up off its foundation, had excavation done, and poured concrete walls for a full basement. A year later, I began a remodeling project to build a two-bedroom apartment down there and was anxious to get it ready to move in to. After working late one evening, I went upstairs and Brenda had a surprise for me.

"Hey, you. Come here." Brenda took my hands and looked at me with loving eyes. "I'm pregnant."

"Whoa! How'd that happen?"

"Well, now, let's see. Do we need to have a little birds-and-bees conversation, honey?"

"Oh, I know. That must have sounded stupid. I'm just surprised. Wonderfully surprised. Wow. We're gonna have a baby!"

Now that Brenda Sweet was pregnant with our first child, I worked even harder on the basement apartment. I was more determined than ever to have a decent place for us all to live. It had been ages since I had seen my girls, and I had no reason to believe that would change until they were of age. I was being given the opportunity to start fresh with a new family.

As Brenda got further along in her pregnancy, people at church asked me, "Are you going to be done in time for Brenda?"

"Oh, sure—just a couple more weeks," I said.

Well, my "couple more weeks" dragged on until we were two weeks away from her due date. And even though I really did think that I could make it in time for our new baby, others knew better.

Then, with barely a week left before Brenda's due date, I was working frantically in the basement when I looked out the window and saw a truckload of men from our church pull up. They came inside and went to work.

An hour after we pounded the last nail and put the last piece of furniture in place, I took my Brenda Sweet to the hospital. I was so hoping for a boy, and everyone in the hallway laughed as I ran from the delivery room screaming, "It's a Ryan, it's a Ryan!" Our gorgeous new son was born March 1, 1988, and the three of us went home to our newly remodeled house.

With the completion of the new living quarters, I found that my appetite for sex intensified, strengthening my desire to express my femininity.

"Hey, sweetie. I'm feeling very girly. Would you mind doing my face up a little before we get started?" I asked.

"Well, okay. But you do know I'm not a lesbian. And remember last time? You felt so silly afterwards," she said.

"I know. But I'm really into it tonight. And that was over three years ago."

"Okay. Sit down over here at my mirror. Let's start with your eyes. So, you've got green eyes. What color eye shadow do you think would look good?"

"Um, green?"

"Exactly. And that's what color eyeliner I'm going to use too."

"Cool. Wow, I'm looking fantastic!"

"Yes, you are. And now, to top it all off, a light red lipstick—there. You're gorgeous, honey."

"Come here." I took her into my arms and kissed her all the way to our bed. I still felt a bit of shame afterward, but it was becoming less intense with time.

I not only had Brenda do me up with makeup to enhance our sex, I also began sleeping in a silky nightgown. I was, of course, terrified that others would find out about my cross-dressing and think of me as some sort of freak, so I continued to stay under the radar.

Three years later, on January 21, 1991, my second son, Brandon, was born and I was every bit as excited with Brandon's arrival as I had been with Ryan's. "Bip Bop and Hey Diddle Diddle" by Paul McCartney was the song for my babies Nicole, Ryan, and Brandon. Michelle, of course, had her own song.

In addition to raising my sons, I got involved with the Christian Right between 1988 and 1992. That's something that today I'm terribly ashamed of and wish I could erase from my history. But I can't.

I was what one would call a black-and-white Christian, a typical if-the-Bible-said-it-that-settles-it type of Christian. I believed that the Bible could be proven to be eighty percent accurate without even talking about religion. As I said in an earlier chapter, I came to that conclusion after I attended a seminar by speaker and author Josh McDowell called *Evidence that Demands a Verdict.*

My only involvement in politics was registering to vote back in 1980 as a Republican. But it wasn't until 1986 that it would matter. I was listening to the news on my clock radio and heard that the liberal incumbent US Senator from Oregon, Bob Packwood, was being challenged in the primary by a conservative Baptist preacher, Joe Lutz. Being a conservative, that really impressed me. I learned that a man named Lon Mabon was behind the Lutz campaign and that Mr. Mabon later formed a group called the Oregon Citizens Alliance.

Lon Mabon decided to file a petition for Measure 8, an initiative that would repeal Governor Neil Goldschmidt's executive order banning discrimination based on sexual orientation in the executive branch of state government. That was the first of Mr. Mabon's political campaigns I was involved in. I traveled to his Wilsonville office to see how I could help. I met him and his wife Bonnie, and found them to be polite, dedicated Christians. He was at the early stages of the campaign and warmly welcomed me into the organization.

Thirty-six counties make up the state of Oregon, and I was made director of the largest one, Multnomah County. My job as director was to organize the signature gatherers and keep track of the signature sheets for my county. I had groups of volunteers getting signatures primarily in the Portland area, and I would also visit friendly churches to solicit their help. As a parent, I was concerned that "homosexual behavior" would eventually become normalized through our schools, and I wanted to keep my kids away from that kind of lifestyle.

We were shown videos of naked gay men on floats as they traveled through the city on Gay Pride day, and that kind of licentious activity scared the hell out of parents like me. I couldn't understand why I was always being called a hatemonger. On one occasion, I was giving a press conference at a downtown hotel in Portland, when a group of angry gay men broke into the room, tossing condoms at us and chanting, "Hatemonger, hatemonger, hatemonger."

I didn't hate anyone. I just didn't want to see my children end up on those floats buck naked and then have someone tell me that sort of behavior was normal and healthy. Even during the campaigns when we used that float footage, gay rights activists would ask, "What about Mardi Gras?" And although I knew they had a point because both parades celebrated sex with nudity, I was simply closed-minded enough not to allow it to sway me, although I couldn't help feeling guilty when complaining about the drag queens. After all, the only difference between them and me was that I was in the closet and in denial.

The right-wingers' concern, including my own, was about a behavior, a lifestyle. It wasn't until I began to come to terms with my own identity in 2011 that I realized how wrong that kind of thinking was. It doesn't matter if you're straight or gay; anyone can be licentious. Identity, on the other hand, is how we identify ourselves in our minds. And from childhood, we're taught to live according to our physical characteristics: our genitalia. Some of us, however, ended up with equipment that didn't match our brain's wiring. It's all about behavior versus identity.

When I made that discovery, I became ill. "What have I done?" I asked myself over and over again. There was a reason those goddamned skinheads followed us around during campaigns. I helped create an environment for hate.

Measure 8 was the only statewide campaign launched by the O.C.A that was successful and passed, 52.7 to 47.3 percent. It was later overturned by the Oregon Supreme Court. That put a new spring in Mabon's step and another campaign, one that would limit abortions performed in Oregon, was launched. Those of us who were pro-life were hopeful for the measure because it didn't seem too intrusive. I don't know whether it was the glory from his statewide victory or his personal religious convictions, but Mr. Mabon added language that was much harsher than many in the Christian community were happy with, including me. The original language included exceptions for rape and incest. Lon wasn't happy with those and removed them. Other leaders in the Christian community chose to launch Measure 10, an initiative that would require a minor to have permission from her parents before getting an abortion. But it wasn't my initiative; it was Lon's. So we all went to work, trying our best to get it on the ballot.

News cameras followed us constantly, and I got a firsthand look at how cameras could change people. Anytime a camera crew came near Lon or other O.C.A. leaders, they behaved differently. Eventually it seemed like many of us, including Lon Mabon, were often played by the media asking loaded questions and/or editing footage just to create headlines. We would be filmed all day and go home expecting to see our hard work on TV, but instead we saw clips taken from awkward moments and aired in a way that created false impressions.

The O.C.A. failed with the initiative to outlaw abortions and went on to another statewide anti-gay initiative, Measure 9. Several Bible verses were relied on for justification of the measure. One was Romans 1:26-27: "Even their women exchanged natural sexual relations for unnatural ones; in the same way, men committed shameful acts with other men and received in themselves the due penalty for their error."

There was a run for governor in 1990 by O.C.A.'s Al Mobley. It also failed. I remained Multnomah County director until 1992, when I started a chapter of Traditional Values Coalition of Oregon and became a lobbyist. I represented the conservative churches in Oregon's state legislature. I spent a lot of time in our state capital, meeting with legislators, speaking for and against various bills as they related to "traditional values."

Way too much of my life was spent working against my own interests. I was wrong—so very wrong—and I'm sorry. There's hardly a day that goes by that I don't feel the shame of my folly. But there it is. I won't try to hide from it. It's all a matter of public record.

Chapter Thirteen

"Brenda, wow—look at this. I have boobs. I've noticed a little growth for a while but just attributed it to a case of 'man boobs.' But wow, look. I'm still growing!" I said.

"Oh, my. I don't know how I didn't notice that before, but you're right. Here, let me grab my measuring tape and let's measure you. Hmm…looks like you're a 38B. You may need to see a doctor. I think you have what they call gynecomastia. I have a friend who said her father had it. Turned out, he began producing estrogen and needed testosterone shots. You may need that, honey." Brenda replied.

"Testosterone shots? I don't like the sound of that. I'm no doctor, but I know that would increase my assertiveness. And you'd be okay with that?

"Hmm. You do have a point there."

"And besides, I kind of like 'em," I said as I turned sideways, looking at my naked profile in the mirror.

"You'll need to start wearing a bra."

"I'm fine with that. I'll just have to wear loose-fitting, baggy shirts so no one will notice."

"You should be okay with only a 38B. But I still want you to see your doctor to make sure there's not something else going on."

"Okay, honey. I'll make an appointment first thing tomorrow."

I went to my doctor's appointment and after a blood draw, my doctor evaluated me and gave me his recommendations. I knew Brenda would want the results as soon as possible, so I went home to discuss them with her.

"Hi, honey. Just saw my doctor, and you were right. I have gynecomastia. He did a blood test and found that my testosterone level is quite low for a male my age and that my estrogen levels are very high, and he recommended testosterone treatment," I said.

"Well. I guess that explains why you've needed Viagra for the last two years too. So what are you going to do? Are there any health concerns?" asked Brenda.

"I asked him if there were any major health risks in staying the course and letting nature take its course, and he said none. And I don't want to take testosterone. I like my female attributes."

"Oh, dear. I know, and I like the softer you too. Well, if there are no health issues, stay the course. We seem to get along better too."

"By the way, I'd really like to have a female doctor now, so I've put in a request for one at Kaiser Sunnyside."

"If that's what makes you comfortable, now's a good time to switch."

I was alarmed and excited at the same time. I wasn't taking hormones or doing anything that could have caused so much growth and was stunned that I needed to wear a bra. I was a little worried about what others might think if they found out I was wearing a bra. Especially my boys. It was 2005; Ryan was seventeen and in high school, and Brandon was fourteen, being home-schooled.

But I was excited as hell too, as I loved the thought of having boobs. I was thrilled that I had Brenda's support in my renewed feminine curiosities and slowly began trading some of my male clothes for more feminine ones. I also started wearing light makeup on special occasions. For my new women's wardrobe, I made all of my purchases online and  only chose clothes that would allow me to remain androgynous. Androgyny ended up making me feel like a freak, though. I was so afraid of standing out, but that's exactly what happened when I wore androgynous clothes.

Brenda was wonderful. She not only helped me with my bra shopping, she also began to invite me to some of her girls-only business meetings.

On our first girls' night out, we attended the October 2005 NW Women's Show. There were mini fashion shows, cosmetic booths, women's-health-related booths, and for those who like a little excitement, a chorus line of firefighters who did a striptease.

I was wearing a teal-green, button-up, size-14 shirt and size-14 slacks. My hair was still short, so even with makeup, I looked like a feminized male. And for those who want to pass as female, that's a terrible place to be.

On our way to the event, I began to have doubts about my clothing decisions.

"Brenda, how do I look? Do I look like a freak?" I asked.

"Of course not, honey! You look wonderful," she said.

Once we made it to the Oregon Convention Center, parked, and made our way inside, I was happy to see the ballroom predominantly filled with other women. Women were, and are, so much more understanding when it comes to gender issues. In my experience, the vast majority of those who disrespect transgender people are male. They seem to feel threatened and simply choose to reject us rather than learn more about us. So I grew to have a deep disdain for many men, especially at social gatherings.

I constantly watched to see if I was being gawked at as we toured the exhibits. For most of my life, I had lived outwardly as a "macho man," and there I was in female mode, terrified that I would end up looking like a complete fool.

"Brenda, look over there. Are those people staring?" I asked.

"Of course not. It's just in your head. Relax," she said.

It's at that stage of transition when many transgender people feel most vulnerable and threatened. We're living with one foot in each world—part male, part female. So yes, at that stage, I did stand out, and people did notice.

We continued through the exhibits, and I struck up conversations with many of the women. Not one of them treated me unkindly or rudely. Every one of them greeted me with a smile and a welcome.

"Hey, sweetie. We better stop here at Taco Bell so you can run in and wash off your makeup before we get home. Both the boys are going to be there, and they'll probably notice," said Brenda.

After we got home from the show, I felt something I'd never felt before—I felt beautiful. "Hey, Brenda, that was fantastic! Those women accepted me with open arms and treated me like one of them, just one of the girls," I said.

"You *were* just like the other girls, silly. And there were other women there who looked androgynous. You weren't the only one. You fit in wonderfully," she said.

That caused my heart to soar. I knew I could never go back to my old self—the wrench-turning macho male who needed to be in control of most everything. I loved the softer me.

Although many women use tools and some are quite strong, I wanted to get away from all of that. I wanted to have hands and legs as soft as a baby's face. I wanted to be welcomed at women-only groups, and I wanted to know what it felt like to have my chair pulled out for me at restaurants, to have my car door opened for me, and so on. And the crazy thing was, never once did I think of myself as a woman. I was just becoming a "softer male" with female attributes.

I could only enjoy my feminine side while attending our women's meetings. At home and at work, I was still Bill Casey.

I spent most of my time at home as more of a domestic partner for Brenda. Brenda, on the other hand, spent her days at our shop. As it turned out, the switch was practical in that Brenda was getting some much-needed training to manage our business, and I began to feel a sense of renewed purpose. Although she had previous experience managing gift and card retail stores, managing a professional working crew in the construction industry was completely different. I was good at keeping the house in order, cooking, cleaning, and just generally taking care of my family.

In December 2005, Brenda and I had our first spa day. We had the works—massage, facial, manicure, and pedicure and I even had a professional makeup job. As usual, I felt a little silly afterward and quickly had it all removed. But as time went on, applying makeup and keeping it on proved to be one of the simpler changes I made.

In 2006, I began taking a number of herbal supplements containing phytoestrogens, hoping they'd enhance my breast growth and lower my testosterone levels even further. But after a couple of months, I found they were a waste of money and didn't do anything. I decided I needed the real thing.

Buying hormones online was easy. There was one small hitch, however: I needed a consultation with a physician. That wasn't much of an issue, as I'd found a website for transgender people that offered everything from basic information to hormones to phone consultations with their doctor.

I made an appointment, and the doctor asked me questions about my sexuality. "So tell me, why are you interested in starting a hormone regimen?"

"I've been taking on many female attributes, and I'm beginning to feel more female than male. I'm happy with these changes and want to enhance them," I said.

"Well, people can call themselves Mickey Mouse, but it doesn't mean that they can become Mickey Mouse," the online doctor said with a chuckle.

Stunned, I quickly hung up on him. This was supposed to be a resource to help people transition? But the first thing I'd gotten from him when I called was a consultation number, which was enough to obtain the hormones. I called the online pharmacy, gave them the number, and ordered a six-month supply of estrogen in every form available. Given that my primary-care physician still didn't cover such treatment, I was on my own for determining which form to take and with what frequency. I found information on estrogen blood-level targets online and went to a private lab to have bloodwork done. It wasn't cheap, but at least I was self-medicating according to safe guidelines. Unfortunately, I began my hormone regimen without first telling Brenda and kept the supplements hidden in my bathroom medicine cabinet. That really was uncalled for, as I had no reason to believe she would oppose what I was doing.

Two months later, she found my stash while she was cleaning. As we were getting ready for bed that night, she brought it up.

"Bill," she asked, "what's this all about? Do you have a prescription for these?"

"No, honey, I don't. I thought I'd save some money by buying them online," I said.

"You know, I've supported you all along in your efforts to become a softer person, she answered, "but I think I'm getting a little stretched. I'm uncomfortable with you just going off and buying hormones online, and to tell you the truth, this 'lesbian lovers' role-playing has me feeling a bit guilty, too."

"Brenda, honey, I'm so sorry. I never meant to make you feel bad. That's it. I quit. No more hormones. No more makeup or clothes. I'm done."

Brenda didn't say anything more, and we both just went to bed. I silently cried myself to sleep. I began the following day feeling sad and withdrawn. I packed all my women's clothing in a box and put it in the garage. I was determined to honor Brenda's feelings, so I did my best to man up for her. The next evening at bedtime, I thought I'd try and give her some "manly" loving.

"Hey, Brenda Sweet, come here," I said. We both undressed and fell on the bed and began passionately kissing. But it was no use. I still needed Viagra to perform, and by then, not even that helped. It certainly wasn't the first time this had happened, and Brenda always understood. That night, however, was different. My hormone pills were gone; Brenda had taken them. My female clothes were stored away. I was back to living a lie. I'd been pretending to be male all my life, and it was killing me. When I was on my hormones and wearing female clothes, I felt happier than I'd ever been. And even though putting the brakes on everything sent me into a deep depression, I wasn't going to live in a way that Brenda found unacceptable.

I returned to work again and pretended that all was back to normal. It was excruciating after finally having gotten a good taste of my female self. During the evenings, I played downer music. Radiohead's "Creep" was on a loop. After a few days, Brenda noticed I wasn't myself and asked to talk with me about it.

"Bill, I can see that you've been miserable, and I don't like it. I liked the way you were before. I just want you to be under the care of a doctor if you're going to be on hormones. And as for the clothes, I didn't expect you to get rid of them. I *am* occasionally uncomfortable, because I'm not a lesbian. But I know it's you—a very feminine you, but a much nicer and softer you. And I like the softer you. So don't worry about me; I'm just adjusting. I want the softer Bill back."

I couldn't believe what I'd heard. In tears, I embraced her and said, "Oh, my Brenda Sweet! I don't deserve you. You've made me so happy. My God, I love you!" I kissed her like it was our first date in 1979.

The next day, I brought my women's clothing out of storage, made an appointment to see a doctor to get a prescription, and started taking hormones again. At that stage of my hormone regimen, my only conscious goal was to lessen my testosterone levels and become a little more feminine. It would be some time later before I discovered my authentic self and begn transitioning to a complete woman—a woman physiologically as well as psychologically.

We were so happy once I was back to myself that we decided to celebrate in Las Vegas. I booked a room in one of the casinos and found out that there was a Beatles tribute band called the Fab Four performing there.

As we began packing for our trip, I asked Brenda, "Hey, honey, do you think I should take any makeup or girly clothes?"

"Sure! No one's going to know you there. Let's have some fun. Go ahead and let your hair down," she said.

When we landed in Vegas, I was awestruck. I'd never been there before and just couldn't believe all the glittering lights, the risqué decor, the ambiance, and the adults-only night clubs with scantily dressed women.

We checked into our room and discovered that the Fab Four were performing that evening, and we could have dinner during the show. Brenda helped me with my makeup, and we went down to enjoy the show.

"Hey, Sweet, look at that dark entrance. It looks just like the original entrance to the Cavern Club," I said. The Cavern Club in Liverpool was where the Beatles first became popular in the UK.

"Oh, yeah. I read in their flyer that the entire cafe has been done up to replicate the Cavern Club as much as possible," she said.We entered the room and noticed the small round tables near the stage, all in a low-lit performance hall. We ordered dinner, and just as I took a bite of rice, "Ed Sullivan" came onstage. With the back of his wrists on his hips, he said, "Good evening, ladies and gentlemen. Tonight's going to be a really, really big show." When he introduced the Fab Four, they walked onstage looking exactly like The Beatles, in 1964.

I had a hard time believing what I was seeing and hearing. They not only made themselves look and sound just like the real deal, they had all their gestures down as well. They sang several of the original songs from the Sullivan Show, such as "She Loves You," "Twist and Shout," and "Long Tall Sally." They did a costume change and came back out and performed "Yesterday," "Michelle," and "Got to Get You into My Life." After one more costume change, out came "Sgt. Pepper's Lonely Hearts Club Band." The music was so perfect I assumed that they were lip-syncing, but I later learned that they actually were singing and playing their instruments.

But the best thing about my trip to Vegas was that no one looked at me twice. There I was, wearing makeup and women's attire, feeling gorgeous and wonderfully liberated, and no one noticed or treated me as anything less than normal.

Chapter Fourteen

On a dark day in the early fall of 2006, my son Ryan left for George Fox University. Brenda and I followed his car to campus, hauling his stuff in our minivan. We planned to stay long enough to get him settled in, attend a parents' meeting, and return home.

When we arrived, I opened the back of the van, and Ryan reached for his electric guitar and said, "Here, Dad. I'll grab that. Follow me. My room is right over there in that building."

When we walked in, I said, "Wow! It's a bit small, isn't it, son?"

Ryan, who had always been a minimalist, chuckled and said, "Well, it's got a bed and a desk. What else do I need?"

After we finished unpacking his things, Brenda and I went to the parents' meeting, then back to his room to say goodbye. I looked him straight in the eyes and said, "I'm going to miss you, son. Now, don't you be a stranger!" Tearing up a little, I grabbed and hugged him.

He looked back at me, and I saw something in his eyes I'd never seen before:

I'm free; I'm independent. In my mind, I heard "I'm Free" by The Who. He hugged me back, flashed his dimpled smile, and said, "Don't worry, Dad; I'll be fine."

I left the campus feeling like I had left a body part behind. I'd never felt that way before, and I wondered if it had something to do with the hormones. Whatever caused it, I didn't see it coming.

Brenda and I didn't talk much when we got home. I didn't sleep well at all and woke up tired. Before she left for work, I said, "Brenda Sweet, I don't think I'm okay with Ryan going away. In fact, I'm really feeling out of sorts."

"I know, honey," she said. "It's going to be an adjustment for me too. But we'll get each other through it. Love you!" She walked out the door and left me alone in the house.

I went into our bedroom and sat on the edge of the bed. I looked up and saw the collage of pictures on the wall that Brenda had assembled of Ryan's life since the day I ran down the hallway shouting, "It's a Ryan! It's a Ryan! It's a Ryan!"

When he was two, I put him up on top of my head, holding his hands and saying, "Ryan, Ryan, where's Ryan?" looking back and forth as if trying to find him.

"I'm right here, Dad! I'm right here!" he'd say with the cutest belly laugh.

There he was at three, smiling his dimpled smile, adding a thumbs-up and a wink. Everybody always loved that.

I thought about when he was sixteen and I taught him to drive. I don't know what possessed me to think that the Columbia Gorge would be a good place to teach him, but that's where we went. I took out the keys to our station wagon and said, "Okay, Ryan, it's all yours. Let's go."

Ryan was still shorter than me, and his head just barely made it over the steering wheel. He started the car and took off flawlessly. He was quiet by nature, and as he drove, he was stone sober and emotionless. I directed him where to go and watched to see that he was using his turn signals. We drove down a single-lane highway and passed my old Job Corps Center. It dawned on me that the roads up ahead got pretty dicey, with their high cliffs and sharp curves with no room to pass. I decided to bite my tongue, and we went on. With anyone else, I would have said something, but Ryan was different. He was beyond his years when it came to common sense, and I wanted to see how he performed under pressure.

We found ourselves on a very narrow stretch of highway with towering cliffs—straight up on one side and straight down on the other. Ryan didn't skip an emotional beat. The entire trip, he remained expressionless, looking straight ahead, taking every one of the many hairpin curves way too fast for me.

"Hey, son, don't you think you're going a bit fast?" I asked, gripping the armrest so hard I loosened it a little.

"Speed limit's twenty-five, Dad. I'm doing twenty-four," he said with a half-smile. Those curves were treacherous, and even at twenty-five, you could make the rubber screech. But he was within the speed limit, so I continued to white-knuckle the armrest while praying for a straight, wide-open road.

Minutes later, I noticed someone's car turned sideways, not moving, right there in the middle of the road, with its inhabitants gathered around it. Visibility was perfect and I thought, *Well. Ryan can certainly see that. I wonder: will he pull over, or will he just go around them?*

Ryan got closer, and he didn't slow down. I shouted, "Ryan, stop!" He didn't say a word. He went around them and chose not to discuss the matter any further. Me? Let's just say that when we got home, I did a quick underwear change.

And then it hit me hard: my baby boy was gone. I wouldn't be seeing his little white car in my driveway anymore, other than for short visits. I should've been happy. Ryan was very well prepared to be on his own. But there would be no more head bounces, no more thumbs up. I sat there and cried in my bedroom as I listened to McCartney tunes. *Damn hormones!*

Ryan settled in well at his new college, and I adjusted to seeing him when he came home for visits.

A few weeks after Ryan's move, Brenda became a member of a women's networking group called Women Entrepreneurs of Oregon in an effort to drum up more business for Casey's Plumbing. One of the benefits was having a dinner meeting with the other women once a month. One particular winter evening, I asked if I could join her.

"Are you sure you want to go, honey?" she asked. "I mean, I don't mind at all, but it's a group made up of women, exclusively for women. I don't know what they'll say."

"I know, I know. Tell you what. Just take me along, and if there's any problem, I'll just leave, and I'll certainly never hold it against you," I said.

"Okay, sweetie, let's get ready and go. But don't say I didn't warn you if it doesn't work out."

I gave her a wink and a smile as we began to get ready. I decided that I would remain in male mode and not wear any makeup for that first meeting. I did wear my androgynous clothing, however: a pair of women's slacks and my teal button-up shirt.

We pulled up to a romantic-looking little building close to the Willamette River. On the way in, I said, "I guess I am a little nervous. I mean, it probably would be embarrassing as hell if they don't let me in."

"Just relax, honey. Everything's going to be fine, and if they don't let you in, I'll skip tonight's meeting and we'll do dinner somewhere else," said Brenda.

It was a quaint little restaurant overlooking the river, and the setting sun cast a reflection on the water that was extraordinary that evening. Meeting or no meeting, my Brenda Sweet and I were going to enjoy ourselves.

We walked up a short flight of stairs that opened into a hallway, where we were met by a couple of members checking people in. Brenda picked up her membership badge and said, "This is my husband Bill, and if there are no objections, he'd like to be a part of the group."

The women at the table looked at each other, then back at Brenda. "Sure, I don't see any problem. Here you go, Bill. Until your membership dues are processed, you'll need to wear this visitor's badge."

"Thank you so much, ladies, and I'm very happy to meet you!" I said, although "happy" didn't describe the euphoria I felt.

I attended on a regular basis and became a volunteer, producing their monthly newsletter. It was wonderful to be a part of a group of other women, but I sometimes felt a little out of place. I stayed on as an active member and hoped that one day my feeling of discomfort would go away.

Casey's Plumbing had grown to the point that by 2007, we needed to find a building and stop operating from our home. We were fortunate to find a decent property close by. That was a few months before I retired from doing service calls personally. Shortly after we moved in, my daughter Nicole came to work for us as one of our dispatchers. It was wonderful having my daughters in my life again after being apart for so many years. It was interesting how the two made it back into my life.

It had been years since I had seen or heard from them. Back in 1992, just before Michelle got married, she became curious about her family and looked me up in the phone book. She called me and asked if she had any brothers or sisters. I invited her over for dinner, where she met Ryan and Brandon, and we spent the evening talking about the old days when she was little. The boys, who were still in grade school, were thrilled to learn that they had a sister and bragged about it at Sunday school. A short time later, Michelle and her fiancé moved to Brookings, where they got married and started a family. Because of the distance, that was the last I saw of her until they moved back to Portland.

Nicole's contact with us came about in a different way. Years after Michelle got in touch, Nicole's mother-in-law encouraged her to contact me. By then, she had my granddaughter, Shaila, and was pregnant with Kayla. It was also around that time that Nicole became unhappy with her job, and Michelle encouraged her to contact me about working at Casey's Plumbing.

Just before retiring as a service technician, I made a call to a home where I was met by two women as I got out of my truck. Both had short brown hair and were dressed in paint clothes. "Hi, I'm Bill, with Casey's Plumbing. What brings me out here today?" I asked.

"I'm Lisa," one of them said, "and I think there's a leak somewhere. I don't see any water, but depending which room you're in, you can hear it running. It's louder in some rooms. It sounds like there's a faucet wide open somewhere."

"No worries, Lisa. Let's go in and check it out."

"Right this way," she said, and led me into the front room. I stopped cold, stunned at what I saw.

"Oh my god, look at that wall. I don't think I've ever seen a more spectacular shade of pink," I said.

She didn't respond, so I followed her into the master bedroom where she asked, "Hear that?"

"As a matter of fact, I do." I looked over at her freshly painted lavender walls. "Oh my, will you look at that? Where do you buy your paint? That is *so* pretty."

Lisa, obviously having to force a smile said, "Right down the street at Bob's Paint. Let's check this other room." She quickly hustled me across the hall to a smaller room. "Now. Hear that? I think it's loudest here. Got any idea where it's coming from?"

That's where I should have put a sock in my mouth about color. "Yes, Lisa. You're right. It *is* loudest in here." I turned my head just enough to see the lime green stripes newly painted on the bright, lemon-yellow walls. "Wow, Lisa, how did you come up with these colors? I'm overwhelmed. They're so beautiful!"

"Okay," she said. "That's it. I'm uncomfortable now. I called for a plumber, not a goddamn art critic. I'm going to call someone else. Please leave. Just leave. Just go." She pointed to the door.

"Oh, Lisa, I'm so sorry," I said.

"No," she said, cutting me off. "Please just go!"

I slithered back to my truck and drove off like a little child who had just gotten a whipping. I couldn't believe what I had just done. I was like a little child in a store with Mommy, seeing candy and toys for the first time, "Oh, Mommy, look, look, pink cotton candy! Oh, Mommy, look, look, a new Barbie doll! Oh, Mommy, look, look…" Oh Mommy, oh Mommy. I behaved like such an idiot. No wonder Lisa kicked me out. I probably scared her to death, but I did discover color. I had never imagined how beautiful certain colors could be.

A few weeks later, it was our twenty-eighth wedding anniversary, and we decided to celebrate on the beach at Lincoln City.

When we arrived at our favorite coastal spot, we checked into a motel and freshened up for some thrift-store shopping. We pulled into the thrift store's parking lot, and I said, "Today

I'd like to go all out—dress, heels, and even a wig if they have one. I'll just point them out, and you buy, okay?"

"Of course, darling! We're going to get all prettied up tonight!" she answered.

I stood on the edge of the men's and women's sections and began to discreetly scope out dresses. The store was old and dimly lit, and the dark 1960s paneling didn't help. There was a dank smell of moldy laundry that came from the back of the store, but none of that mattered when I saw the dress.

"Brenda," I whispered. "Look at that gorgeous pink gown. Will you hold it up for me?"

Brenda held it up and asked, "Well, what do you think?"

"Wow. It looks perfect. Will you put it in the cart along with these pink pumps? And look over there in the back. There's a box marked 'wigs,'" I whispered.

We looked through the box. It was behind a row of clothes where no one could see me as I scouted for a keeper.

"Wow! Check it out, sweetie," I said. "Long, blonde? What do you think?"

"Oh, perfect. You'll look so elegant in that, along with the gown and pumps," she said.

I noticed that there were some blind spots in the store where no one could see me and decided I'd have a little fun. I picked out several slinky teddies and held one up against my breasts. "Woo-hoo! Look at this, Brenda Sweet. What do you think?" I asked with a wink. We both laughed. The teddy I held wasn't my style at all and looked hilarious. There was barely enough material to cover the nipples, and then it made a V shape where it went down and made a poor attempt to cover the crotch! Hardly more than two handkerchiefs worth of material.

We found exactly what we wanted and went up to the cashier, and Brenda paid for it. And the killer part was that everything together came to less than five dollars.

Our plan was to do my makeup, put on my new wig and clothes, have dinner, do some hot tubbing out on the deck and, and then…

We pulled into the parking lot, and I looked over at Brenda; she gave me one of her sultry looks that said, "Tonight's the night," without speaking a word. I felt my blood pressure rise as we entered our room.

Brenda told me to prepare for my makeup. After I washed my face, she applied a light cover-up for blemishes and to provide a base for the primary makeup. Next, she took out a little application sponge and applied the beige. She followed this with a dusting of golden foundation powder applied with a large fluffy brush to set everything, then applied two tones of blush to my upper cheekbones. After all that, we still needed to do my eyes. Because I have green eyes, she drew dark green liner on my upper and lower eyelids, lengthened my lashes with some dark brown mascara, and completed it all with a light green eye shadow and lipstick.

I was anxious to see myself and went to the bathroom mirror. As I looked at myself, I got chills and my eyes teared up. In the mirror was a beautiful and elegant woman, and I loved what I saw. It had nothing to do with sex—I was looking at me, the real me, the authentic me.

Brenda smiled at me and said, "C'mon, honey. Let's have dinner."

She led me to the table, and we looked at each other like two lovers reunited after a very long separation. Something was changing. That certainly wasn't the first time I dressed up and wore makeup, but it was perhaps the first time in my life I began to let my inner walls come down. That night I began to accept myself for who I truly was: a beautiful woman with feelings I had never before experienced. A beautiful woman with an even more beautiful wife.

I dabbed away my happy tears and went out on the deck to prepare the hot tub. After I got the water up to temperature, we both undressed, stepped into its roiling waters, and, holding hands, we sat down to stare into each other's eyes.

"You've made me so happy," I said, pulling her against me. "I love you so much!"

Brenda took me into her arms, pressing her breasts against mine. "Oh honey, I love you too," she said, and kissed me. "Let's go back inside."

She led me to the bed, lay me on my back, and made love to me. We climaxed at the same time and held each other until we fell asleep in each other's arms.

I had music quietly playing in the background, and as we drifted off, one of my all-time favorite love songs, Paul McCartney's "Motor of Love," came on.

"I can't get over your love
No matter how hard life seems
There's a light in my dreams
Thanks to you

My friends keep asking me why
There's such a smile on my face
There's a home at my place

Thanks to you
Thanks to you."

CHAPTER FIFTEEN

"That's great, it starts with an earthquake,
Birds and snakes, an aeroplane,
Lenny Bruce is not afraid,...
It's the end of the world aswe know it,
It's the end of the world as we know it.
And I feel fine"

R.E.M.

That day, as Ryan stood on the stage I'd built for him in a field and performed the song, I felt more than fine. I felt proud.

He was on summer break from college and performing a concert for his friends. Although he wasn't a professional musician, he could play the guitar and sing well. I was able to help him by throwing together the portable stage for him and his bandmate, Laura. I set up thirty folding chairs and was surprised later to see that all of them were filled, with people standing.

Ryan arrived forty-five minutes before show time to practice and do a sound check. His hair looked like John Lennon's when it was long, and he was wearing his favorite light blue jacket. He performed several songs flawlessly but it was the R.E.M. song that I enjoyed most.

He performed the fast-paced song wonderfully, with witty jokes between songs. He had us all rolling in laughter as we rocked to his roll. Ryan's "Summer Concert in the Field" was a smash hit as far as I was concerned. Clearly, there were two music people in my family, and it was wonderful to connect with him at that level.

Neither he nor his brother Brandon had any idea I was living as a feminized male and taking hormones. I knew I'd have to tell them sometime, but I was nowhere near that time yet. For one thing, my hormone regime was unstable.

Brenda had become friskier than I had ever seen her. So I made a decision, once again, to stop all hormones and give up my feminine clothes. And just like the last time, after a week or so, neither she nor I liked the results. I became depressed and moody with the slightest provocation. Brenda decided we needed to talk.

"Look, I understand what you're trying to do," she said. "I respect that. But I loved you just like you were. And there's a hell of a lot more to a relationship than intercourse. Besides, there's other ways we can have sex, and just like the last time you dropped everything, you're moody and an ass to be around. So c'mon. Get back with the program. We'll be fine."

It was a relief to get back on track and feel normal again. During my entire history of becoming a softer person, I was always sensitive to Brenda's attitude and personal needs. But that wasn't the last time that scene played out. That first year and a half, I started and stopped my hormone regime five times. And each time, Brenda and I would agree that a transition toward femininity was the best course for both of us.

In May of 2010, I began to stockpile hormones. I purchased them on the Internet and had a huge supply of estradiol for injections, along with hypodermic needles and Estrofem tabs and patches. Injections were said to be the safest, although I experimented with patches and tablets as well. I kept the stash, along with some choice lingerie, in a white, thirty-two-gallon garbage bag in my bedroom closet. Even though I had seen a doctor for my prescriptions, they still weren't covered by my insurance, so I continued to get them online to save money.

The site that proved most helpful was transgendercare. com. There I found all I needed in terms of what to take, how much to take, and how to administer everything. Giving oneself a shot in the gluteus can be a bit awkward, and one day I inadvertently stabbed the needle directly into a nerve. Talk about pain. It was sore for months and it left a black bruise.

Later that spring, it was time for another one of our contractor conventions in Houston. I took my shot, put my silky nighties in my hormone bag, reorganized the closet so it was less visible, and packed for my trip. I called Brandon in to tell him that his mother and I would be gone for a few days and he would be on his own. I was a bit squeamish, as we had never left him by himself before. But he was nineteen years old and I thought it was about time to see how he handled a little more responsibility.

"Okay, son, we're going to be gone for three days. Are you sure you'll be able to handle everything? Still got your emergency phone numbers? And can I trust you to not throw any wild parties while we're gone?"

"Whoa, Dad, chill! Everything's going to be fine. Don't worry!" said Brandon.

After exchanging hugs, Brenda and I left for the airport. I was a little nervous with my 38B bra on under my suit. If the TSA noticed it, I'd die of embarrassment. And then there was the silky nightgown in my luggage.

As it turned out, however, the trip turned out to be rather uneventful. We went through security with no problem, and I slept well and undisturbed in my silky nightie. But I couldn't keep my mind off Brandon. I began to have second thoughts about leaving him home alone from the moment we were en route. So when Saturday came and it was time to check out, I was ready.

When we got home, I noticed that our basement windows were wide open. *Oh shit, I hope this isn't what it looks like!* I thought. I rushed in the house and went straight to my bedroom closet to see if my hormone bag had been disturbed. When I entered the room, the first thing I noticed was my expensive, special-order iPhone clock radio was missing and the entire room looked like it had been rummaged through. My heart dropped when I opened my closet door. The white bag with girly clothes and hormones was gone. Just then, I heard a vacuum running upstairs.

I ran up the stairs and screamed, "Brandon! What the fuck happened? Where is the bag I had in my closet and my clock radio?"

I had never felt so violated. Brenda was the only one who knew about my feminine clothing and hormones. It felt like my secret life had been pinned up on our clothesline outside for all the world to see.

"Okay, okay, calm down," Brandon said. "I'm sorry. I invited a friend over for a small party, and he took it upon himself to invite these gangster-type guys and things just got out of hand. They were older, and they were scary. I took your bag and hid it in my room so they couldn't get it. I was really hoping to have everything cleaned up by the time you got home. I'm sorry, Dad."

I began to feel terrible about the way I'd screamed at him. Sure, it was his fault for having a party when he said he wouldn't, but the little bastard he invited over was the real asshole. And because I was missing an expensive collectors' edition clock, I decided to pay a visit to the guy's apartment.

He lived in a poor section of town I'd lived in when I was young. When I pulled into his driveway, the first things I noticed were rows of white, run-down, two-story buildings with most of the paint falling off and cockeyed screen doors, many of them hanging on only one hinge.

When I got to his apartment, I could hear him inside talking with somebody. I knocked on his door, but he didn't answer. I knocked a little louder, and he still ignored me. With the song "Gonna Raise Hell" by Cheap Trick playing in my head, I yelled, "Hey, you little bastard. Get your ass out here! You and your buddies ripped me off, and we need to talk about it."

He opened a window and yelled, "I don't know what you're fucking talking about. Now get out of here or I'm calling the police!"

It was clear that the little hoodlum wasn't going to fess up about anything. If I'd kept yelling, I'd probably have gotten into trouble, so I gave up and left. When I got home, I apologized to Brandon for using such foul language and for screaming the way I did. I felt awful for blowing up so loudly. I chose not to discuss the contents of that white bag with him. I could only assume that he probably already knew and was protecting my secret from his friends that evening. I felt I needed to talk with Brenda too.

"Hey, honey. I'm sorry for getting so loud with Brandon. I haven't cussed out loud like that in ages, and now I feel terrible."

"I know, and you did it outside in our driveway! Our neighbors heard," said Brenda.

"Okay, rub it in. But wow, I don't ever want to get that angry again. It's just that I felt so violated."

"Oh, I know. But you did apologize. How's Brandon feeling now? I'm sure he forgave you."

"Oh, yeah. Of course. I just wish I could take it all back. That's the thing with words; once they leave your lips, they're out there. There's no getting 'em back."

"Hey, I have something to make you feel better. Next month Merle Norman is offering free makeovers at their Lloyd Center store. Wanna come with me for a full makeover?

"Makeup, in the store, in public?" I said.

"Oh, I'm sure they have a place set back a little from public view. So what do you say? Wanna come with me?"

"Sure, I guess. I mean, as long as I'm not directly in the public view."

I not only got my makeover, but I actually found the confidence to leave with the makeup on. We left the salon and walked down the street to the Claim Jumper Restaurant for dinner.

"Right this way, ladies," said the host as we entered the restaurant.

That really got my confidence going the right direction. There were only a few other couples there at that time and a man by himself, sitting directly across from me. From the moment I sat down, I could feel him looking at me. He was a middle-aged man with short graying hair, wearing a plaid wool jacket.

"Hey, Brenda. Don't look directly at him, but do you see that man across from me? I think he's staring at me. Is he?"

"Well, he *is* looking in this direction," she said, trying to be discreet.

He was still watching us when the food came, and I said, "Hey, Brenda Sweet, that guy is definitely staring at me."

Brenda looked directly at him. "You're right. He's staring at you nonstop."

I saw a look in his eyes of seething hate. He continued to stare the entire time I was in the restaurant. A part of me was pissed and wanted to stare back, but I was more humiliated than angry and chose to ignore him.

When we left the restaurant, I made every effort to avoid trouble. I felt far more vulnerable in public after that—at least while I was still living as an androgynous male.

That same summer, Brenda helped me find an adorable outfit to wear at home: a light purple skirt with a black top. She even found me a lacy apron to wear when I was in the kitchen. I then had higher estrogen levels than most females my age and was totally comfortable wearing feminine clothing in my own home. I was becoming a much softer person, and it seemed like all the recent changes were just a natural course of events for me. However, at no time did I ever sit down and think, *Gee, I think I want to start living as a female.* I was just changing—changing in ways that were remarkable to others but so wonderful and natural to me. In addition to having boobs, I found that my hips were enlarging while my upper-arm and muscle mass was shrinking, becoming leaner and much weaker. The hormones certainly accounted for some of the changes, but again, my breasts had been developing well before I began taking estrogen.

For the first time, I attended a Women Entrepreneurs of Oregon meeting wearing makeup. Unfortunately, it felt awkward. I had short hair and was wearing a pair of women's slacks and a shirt, with my face totally done up. I guess it was no surprise that I got a lot of stares. Although I was a long-time member of the women-only group, I had always before attended as a male. But no one said anything unkind, nor did anyone treat me any differently.

My confidence had grown, and even though it felt awkward at first, I started to wear light makeup in public more and more often. The one exception was in my business. No one had any idea of my changes back at the shop, and I was determined to keep it that way.

In addition to makeup, I began to experiment with acrylic nails. Maintenance was a bit of a nuisance, however, as I needed fills about every three weeks to keep up with nail growth. Eventually, fake nails became a necessity. During one of my killer salad preps, I accidentally chopped into my thumbnail, and the acrylic nail was necessary to cover it. So going to the shop was more of a challenge than ever. I ended up making fewer appearances there, and when I did go, I wore rubber gloves to hide my pretty nails.

One Monday morning, I pulled into the driveway of Casey's Plumbing, hoping to run in, grab a document I needed, and get back out before anyone noticed me. Nicole was the only person who would be there, and she would be back in the dispatch office, well out of view of my office. But wouldn't you know it, Nicole was in the kitchen when I arrived, and I would have to walk right past her with my new nails.

"Oh, hi, sweetie! How are you?" I discreetly grabbed a pair of rubber gloves on a shelf next to the entrance.

"Hi, Dad. Everyone's working. Doing okay. How about you?

"I'm fine. I just stopped in to pick up the Steven's bid. We're going start this job next week."

"Great. Glad we got it. I'll put it on the schedule."

"Thanks, honey. See you later." I left and absentmindedly drove home still wearing my rubber gloves.

"Hi, honey. What's up with the rubber gloves? Doing some cleaning?" asked Brenda.

"No, no. I stopped in at the shop to grab a contract and bumped into Nicole. I wasn't expecting to see her, but fortunately, these gloves were handy. I slid them on before she could notice my nails," I said with a laugh.

"Wow. Sounds like a close call. Well, I was just leaving for work. See you later," Brenda replied.

"Hey, let's go out for dinner tonight. I want to do something fancy downtown to make up for the Claim Jumper. I'm sure I can find something safe downtown. What do you say?"

"Sure. Sounds like a great idea."

By evening, I was feeling especially romantic and reserved a table for us at the Portland City Grill, with its sweeping views of the downtown. I wore exactly what I wore at the

Claim Jumper: slacks, button-up shirt, short hair, and makeup. The only difference was my acrylic nails. So I was pleased when they greeted us with, "Ladies, please come this way." Those of us living in-between desperately need moments like those. Brenda and I sat across from each other at a small table, holding hands. I felt myself falling in love with her all over again and hoped the night would last longer.

I began to add more women's clothes to my wardrobe, experimenting with skirts and dresses. I was stunned at the variety of clothes to choose from, and for the first time in my life, I completely understood why so many women loved to shop and never seemed to have enough clothes. Although at one time there had been an element of sexual excitement in wearing women's clothing, those days were gone. I simply felt natural and comfortable. I felt more female than male and decided I would never go back.

Chapter Sixteen

On Valentine's Day, 2011, I bought Brenda a pink card that read, "To My Lovely Wife." She opened it and put her hand over her mouth, laughing. Puzzled, I asked, "What? What are you laughing at? That's not a funny card."

She handed me the card she bought for me. I opened it and saw that it was the exact same card. Even though I had changed in so many ways, our minds were still intertwined. I grabbed and hugged her as we laughed together.

Later that month, at one of our WEO meetings, my friend Tia approached me and said something that changed my life.

"Okay, Bill, so how far are you going to take this?"

"What?" I asked, rattled at what I'd just heard.

"So, what's it going to be, Bill?" she asked.

I stammered a bit, not really knowing what to say. After all, I had never really planned to actually become a woman, not totally anyway—I just wanted female attributes. But there I was, in full bloom—an androgynous male at worst, a beautiful female at best. So I replied, "Oh, Tia, not to worry. It will never go beyond this—I mean; you'll never see me show up in a dress."

Her question made me realize that I really had come a long way—and yet, she was the only one who said anything. So I was a little embarrassed and wasn't sure she approved.

Of course, I had no idea how incorrect my "never show up in a dress" comment would ultimately become. And it must be noted, those sweet WEO friends had not only accepted me fully as I was, but also offered me leadership positions just as I was, male or otherwise.

That night, when I told her about Tia's comments, Brenda looked me straight in the eyes and said, "Bill, you *are* a woman!"

I'd never actually thought that myself, but after all I had been through, maybe they were right. "Me? A woman?"

"Yes, Bill. Look at your history. You've been living as a woman for months now. And really, don't you think it's time to say it out loud?"

I began to tear up and took Brenda into my arms. "Oh, Brenda. I love you. Of course you're right. God knows how long I've been repressing all this. Thank you. Thank you!"

It seemed that even though I'd yearned to embrace my femininity from a very young age, I was blind to what others saw in me. Indeed, Brenda and Tia not only saw, but were gracious enough to open my eyes to the obvious: I was—I *am* a woman.

It was so wonderful to finally be me. The authentic me. Although still physically male, my bloodwork revealed that my estrogen levels were still higher than those of most women my age. My androgynous clothes were still in-between and I began to wear makeup almost everywhere in public, except at our shop.

A week later, I had a dental appointment and thought, *Yes, I'm going there as my true self.* I wore women's clothing and makeup. At the check-in desk, it was awkward and beautiful at the same time. I handed them my membership card, and they looked at it for the longest time, like they were trying to see right through it, then back up at me, back to my card— and then the most wonderful thing happened. They began referring to me as "she." I turned around and felt my eyes welling up as a supervisor came out and invited me into her office to "discuss the situation."

"So what's up, Casey?" she asked. "You've been a patient here for years, and we've never seen you dressed like this before."

"I completely understand how shocking this must be for you," I said. "I mean, I've been going through these changes gradually for years, and today I have finally accepted that I am a transgender woman, and now I identify as such. But yes, for you and others who haven't witnessed the transition, I can certainly see how it would be a surprise."

"No problem, Casey, and actually, I'm quite happy for you. I'll see to it that the staff knows what they need to know, and we'll do our best to respect and support you in this."

On the way out, the desk clerk—a man in his thirties, leaned toward me and said, "I think you're going to make a gorgeous woman."

It was all I could do to get to my car, where I cried tears of happiness and joy.

Things were rapidly coming together at that point. We'd been members of a very conservative church for most of our married life and had grown close to several members. I was at a point where I wore a bra under my suit and eventually, even light makeup. Which was remarkable given my shameful right-wing activism, nineteen years earlier in 1992. But it was who I was and I was comfortable—that is, until one of the elders came over to say hello one Sunday morning and leaned way down into my face, as if trying to see if he saw what he thought he saw.

"Hey, Brenda, here comes Tim. Think he'll notice my makeup?" I whispered to Brenda.

"I don't know, honey. It's so light, it's really hard to notice. He'd have to get right down face to face, and we're several seats in from the aisle. He won't want to climb over people. Don't worry, you're safe," she said.

Not!

Tim was a very friendly elder. I looked up, and there he was, climbing over couple after couple, shaking their hands along the way—working his way to me.

"Hey, Bill. How are you?" said Tim as he worked his way past the last couple to greet me, face to face. After getting his close-up, his eyes popped open in astonishment, and he stopped just short of saying, "Wow!" Clearly, he was stunned when he saw my makeup.

There was another elder, Brad, whom I had come to think of as the father I never had. Even though he had a scientific and logical mind, the studies I provided him about transgender people didn't teach him anything. When I spoke to him on the phone, he said, "I was fine with a son; I don't need another daughter." So that was that. I was deeply hurt, and had it been anyone else, I probably would have cried. But

I knew Brad well and his response really was no surprise. Indeed, it was "quite logical."

After all the years as active members, we left. Over time I became disillusioned with churches and organized religion. Oh, I still pray and encourage others to do so as well. I just won't refer to mainline theologies or quote Bible verses.

It felt strange to not be attending church anymore. After all, for thirty years we attended two to three times a week. But having all that free time gave me time to think about who I was. One thing was clear; my ID was wrong, and I decided to talk to Brenda about it. We were in our bedroom when I brought it up.

"Hey, honey. Now that I am indeed a woman, at least undercover, I think it would be appropriate to have a woman's name. How do you feel about that?" I asked.

"I think you're exactly right. But what are you talking about—changing your driver's license?"

"Actually, I would be changing every document with my name on it, including my birth certificate."

"Your birth certificate? You can change your birth certificate?"

"I don't know about other states, but you can here in Oregon."

"Boy. That sounds like a lot of work. Will it be expensive?"

"It will be a bit of work, but it shouldn't cost too much. I want to hire an attorney to handle my name change; that'll be a few hundred dollars, and the rest is basically just paperwork."

"Have you considered any possibilities for a name yet?"

"As a matter of fact, I have. I thought I'd keep my first name simple. People have called me Casey my entire life, so why not just make that my new first name? And I looked it up online, there are thirty-two different ways to spell Casey—I like Caisie the best."

"Oh, that is nice. How about a middle name?"

"Breen. I was looking for a good Irish name, and that one just jumped out at me when I saw it."

"Caisie Breen Casey—very nice. I love it. So, what ID are you going to change?"

"I'd like to change it all. My driver's license, birth certificate, everything. Which brings up another issue. If I'm going to get a new driver's license, I can't have one with that little 'm' for male on it. And Oregon has a law that requires some form of body modification to change gender markers. I could get a simple orchiectomy to meet that requirement. You know, where they clip my nuts."

"That is a big move all right. I suppose it shouldn't matter; I mean, it's not likely we're going to have any more children. But still, surgery is a big deal. Have you talked with a therapist?"

"I have an appointment to see one next week. And seeing a therapist—that's also one of the requirements."

"I think I'm a bit torn. I can see how a name change would be the next order of business for you, but surgery? Can I reserve my thoughts until after you've seen the therapist?"

"Of course! I understand."

I couldn't blame Brenda for being a little reserved about my orchi. She had been supportive of my girly activities from the time we first met and even now supported a legal name change. But going under the knife is another matter, and I respected her feelings of apprehensiveness.

I spent two hours with my therapist the following week and she asked me some simple questions that caused me to fall apart in her office. I told her about my previous right-wing activity, and she simply asked me how I felt about it today. I tried to answer but became overwhelmed with tears and began crying.

"What a fuckin hypocrite! I was a leader in the OCA for two years, I fought against gay rights—I was a cross-dresser for part of that time. Now I discover I'm trans. I worked against my own. God only knows how many I've hurt," I said between tears.

My therapist was kind and listened until I was finished. She assured me that my sadness would eventually go away and diagnosed me with gender dysphoria, thus giving the green light for my procedure. But the shame and sadness I felt when I came face to face with my hypocrisy would go with me for years.

"Hi, honey. I saw that therapist this afternoon, and she diagnosed me with gender dysphoria," I said.

"I guess that means she approved your surgery?" Brenda replied.

"Indeed it does, but I'm not doing anything without your approval."

"Oh, honey. You know I'll support you. I just needed to know that we're moving forward with professionals," said Brenda.

"Thank you, sweetie. I love you so much!"

The attorney I hired to handle my name change said she was in the process of challenging the surgery requirement to change gender markers, and asked me if I wanted to be part of the suit. But I was afraid her court case might take a while, so I declined. Amazingly, it didn't take that long. I learned that a short time after my procedure, she had prevailed, and that surgery was no longer needed to change one's gender marker on his or her ID.

Just days after coming to an agreement with Brenda that my ID needed to be changed, I had a breakdown at Costco when I took my groceries through the checkout. I was dressed in my androgynous mode.

"May I see your ID, please?" asked the checker.

She was a short, middle-aged woman who had to squint, even with her glasses, to see well, as that was what she was doing with my ID. She looked at it, then up at me, then she picked up a microphone and called for the manager.

"Bob, please come to register nine."

Here's one thing people need to understand about those of us in transition. Many of us acquire emotions we've never before experienced. I began crying like a baby. I was so humiliated and embarrassed. And once I started, it was almost impossible to stop. It felt like the entire store was watching, and I wanted to crawl in a hole and die. When the manager finally showed up, I couldn't talk, but he was kind and understanding.

"Hi, Betty. Let's see what you have there," he said as he took my ID. He then looked at me, then back at Betty.

"Everything's fine, Betty," he said and left.

The cashier seemed embarrassed and kept saying, "Oh, I'm so sorry, I didn't know. I'm so sorry." I was more desperate than ever to correct my ID.

After some research, I located a doctor who could do my orchiectomy (orchi for short). He had a six-month waiting list, but I was able to schedule the procedure for January 20, 2012.

Then, there was a small glitch. Brenda and I were enjoying ourselves in Newport one weekend, walking behind a small group of senior citizens, when I decided I wanted to pick up the pace a little to pass them. All of a sudden I felt my chest seize up and had to hold onto a garbage can to remain standing. My strength left as quickly as I could take a deep breath. Brenda had to walk up a hill to get our car and come back down for me. After we got back to Portland, I saw my doctor and discovered that I had angina. Given that my surgeries were a bit down the road, they said I should be all right if I took the medications they prescribed. I began the pill regimen without fail and never missed a dose.

In July, Brenda's grandfather Cecil died.

I wore light makeup and androgynous clothes to his funeral despite my self-consciousness. I was nervous about what

Brenda's family would think, but I also thought perhaps no one would notice because my makeup was so light. The day after the service, we found out that one of his great-granddaughters had asked her grandmother, "Why was Bill wearing makeup?" Her response was, "I don't know, but that's his business if that's what he wants to do."

That grandmother was Brenda's Aunt Melanie, and I couldn't have been happier with the way she handled her granddaughter's question. If that was an indication of how Brenda's family was going to receive my new femininity, I would have little to worry about going forward.

The following week, we planned a coming-out day in Seattle, a progressive city where nobody knew me. The plan was to spend a day in town wearing a pretty dress.

We started the day before at The Bra Boutique. Although I was only a 38B, I was so proud and indeed felt beautiful as I squeezed my breasts together and shook them back and forth and giggled with Brenda. Once we got home and packed, she had some advice about my walk.

"Caisie, I think I'd better give you a little crash course," she said. "Your steps are much too wide. Ladies don't walk that way. Here, watch me. See, knees close together and take small steps. You don't need to be in a hurry. There, now you try it."

"Oh. Okay," I said, and proceeded to walk across the dining-room floor, focusing on keeping my knees together while taking short steps.

"Good, good, that's right, good," said Brenda.

"Thanks, sweet, yeah, I got…oh shit," I said as I tripped over my own feet.

"Oh no, honey. Are you all right?"

"Yes, I'm fine," I said with a laugh. "By the way, how was I doing? I mean, before I fell."

"Actually, you did great. You walk like that and wear the clothes you've picked out, and you won't have any problem at all passing in Seattle."

"Thanks, sweetie. That makes me feel great," I said, and gave her a thank-you kiss.

When we got to our Seattle hotel room the next day, I began to prepare for my big night. Although I had worn women's clothes in public before, I'd never worn a dress or a full face of makeup. But that night, I applied pink eye shadow, dark mascara, and ruby-red lipstick. For the finishing touch, I put on a long black gown and a rope of pearls.

"Okay, honey," I said. "How do I look?"

"Seriously? Dangerously gorgeous. Really, dear, you look wonderful. Let's go," Brenda said.

Across the street from our hotel was a posh-looking little Italian restaurant, and we took our chances on finding a table without a reservation. I was especially pleased when we entered and the waiter said, "Welcome, ladies. Right this way."

Wow, I thought. *So far so good.* He led us to a cozy spot in the back, and I was even more charmed when he pulled the chair out for me to sit. He handed us our menus and quietly walked away.

"Oh my god, Brenda. 'Welcome, ladies!' And he pulled my chair out! I must be looking pretty good. So what do you think? Am I passing?"

"C'mon, dear. You said it yourself. He just referred to us both as 'ladies' and then pulled out your chair. What do you think?"

"You're right, and that was wonderful, but look at that couple over there. Are they staring at me?"

Without a doubt, this is the hardest place to be during a transition, especially for those of us who wait until much later in life to do so: always asking, "Do I pass? How do I look?" The reality was that I did look gorgeous and every bit as natural as the other women there.

"Staring at you?" asked Brenda. "Caisie, you're a gorgeous woman, and the people who are staring are just checking you out. Now you know what we go through. But really, honey, you should be flattered."

I was flattered once I began to feel more comfortable in my new body. The euphoria of living as a woman almost full-time was sometimes more than I could handle. When we left Seattle the next morning, I had a huge, confident smile on my face.

There I was, living almost full-time as a woman, taking steps to change all my IDs—and yet, there were still so many people I hadn't told. Because my sons and I were so close, I felt I needed to tell them first. Although, I did wonder about Brandon. Two years earlier, he had found my bag of hormones, and even though we didn't talk, *surely he must have pieced things together,* I thought.

When Ryan came home for a visit one weekend, I said, "Hi, son. Pull up a chair, will you? I have something important to talk to you about."

"Sure, Dad. What's up?"

"This is really hard, and it's going to sound abrupt, but I don't know any other way to say it. Son, I've been struggling with gender issues for years. No one but your mother has known anything, but I've discovered that I'm transgender. I'm a woman living in a man's body."

"Wow. That's crazy. Are you seeing a doctor? Does Mom know?'

"Great questions son, and yes; I've seen a doctor and I have your mother's full support. And, I'm planning to have a surgery and get a legal name change. Is this something you're going to be okay with, son?"

"Well, I am surprised, and this is huge, but as long as Mom is supportive. And I believe sex is nonbinary anyway. Have you got a good doctor? Have you checked them out?"

"Well, yes. I found a doctor online, and he seems to have a good reputation. Thanks, son, for your support and understanding," I said, and I gave him a big hug while crying some happy tears. I decided to visit Brandon at school the following weekend and tell him in person. He had become a student at Oregon State University and moved in on a weekend I was out of town.

I made the two-and-a-half-hour drive to Corvallis and began to search for his dorm. I'd never been there before and was surprised at how large the campus was. After a diligent search, I found his building and went in to find his room—for some reason, he wasn't answering his cell phone. Finally, I found his room, and the door wasn't closed all the way. I opened it a little, looked inside, and saw a small unmade bed, a very small fridge on the floor, and a pile of books, but no Brandon.

Disappointed, I went back to my car, where I tried calling him again. He answered and said, "Don't go anywhere, Dad. I'll come right out to your car."

Brandon and I had a relationship that was a little different from my relationship with Ryan, who was always more of the logical type. It was easy to explain things to Ryan. Brandon, on the other hand, was more like me, with a big heart and strong feelings. So when I began to tell him, he was more taken aback than Ryan was. Brandon didn't see it coming at all.

"Hey, son. How are you?" I said.

"I'm fine. I was having lunch the first time you called and had my phone off. So how are things at home? How's Mom?"

"Everything's fine, your mother is doing well. She's working more at the shop now."

"So why'd you drive all the way down here when I'll be home on break in a few weeks anyway?"

"Well, ah—it's because I have something important to talk to you about, so important, I need to do it face to face and I can't wait a few weeks."

"Oh. Sounds heavy. Did somebody die?"

"No, nobody died. What I'm about to tell you is probably going to shock you. But let me ask you; remember when you were small and your brother talked you into walking into my bedroom as your mother and I were going to bed, and you saw me wearing a woman's nightgown?"

"Ah, yeah."

"Okay. Now, let's fast-forward to a couple years ago when you had that wild party. Remember that white garbage bag with medical supplies and ladies' sleepwear inside that you retrieved from my closet and hid from the bullies at your party?"

"Yes."

"Do you know what the medical supplies were?"

"No."

"Why do you think I had women's sleep garments in my closet?"

"Hey, it was none of my business. I just didn't want my friends to know."

"Son, do you know what transgender means?"

"I know they say it's when someone has a brain of the opposite sex from their genitalia."

"Brandon, I've seen a therapist, and I've been struggling with gender dysphoria for years. I was born physically male, but my brain was wired female. I've finally surrendered to the conflict in my brain and will be changing my name, and I'll be having surgery."

"Jesus, Dad. I don't know. How do we know that all this 'trans' information is accurate? I don't know; I just don't know," he said, looking down.

"Hey, buddy. I know this is hard for you. No worries. It is a big deal; you're not required to just automatically give me your approval. I'm gonna love you and be here for you no matter how you feel about my change."

"Oh, Dad. I'll be in your corner. But you were right. It is a bit shocking.

It took a little longer to get him to fully understand. He did give me his blessings before I left, but I could see that it would take more time for the information to really settle in for him. And, really, how in the world could I blame him? All his life we had been so close, doing guy things like building forts and skate ramps, while Ryan was always holed up in his room reading and learning computer programming. I loved both boys more than anything, and I would certainly be patient with Brandon's coming to terms with my decision. And Brandon did eventually come to accept and respect my new life.

After I told my sons, I knew I had to tell my other family members and my employees. Because I was beginning to lose body mass and wearing a bra, I wore loose-fitting clothes that made it all but impossible to notice. If people noticed anything, they kept it to themselves, as no one ever said anything to me. Nicole found out by accident. I hadn't really planned my coming-out date, but she came by my house unexpectedly and saw me partially made up as Caisie Breen.

I was getting ready to leave, and Brenda had taken something out to the car while I was still doing my makeup. Then the doorbell rang, and I thought she had locked herself out.

"Lock yourself…" I stopped short when I saw Nicole and froze. I just looked at her with eyes that must have said, "Oh God, help me," because she just smiled and said, "I'll talk to Brenda. Bye."

"See you later, hun," I said in what felt like a slow-motion film clip. My heart sunk.

Later that day, I called Nicole at home. "Hi, honey. Hey, I'm embarrassed as hell. I need to tell you something. I probably should have talked about this earlier, but frankly, it's only been recently that I've begun to understand what's going on myself."

"Oh, hey, you don't owe me any explanation. You're an adult, and you two are entitled to your privacy. What you do in your own house is nobody's business but yours."

"That's sweet, and I appreciate it, Nicole, but I think you may have the wrong idea here. What you saw was me coming to terms with my real self. Over the last several years, I've been going through changes. I'm transgender. Do you understand that term?"

"I think so. Isn't it someone who was born with the wrong body and has the mind of the opposite sex?"

"Exactly! I was born a male physically, but my mind was wired female. It's taken me years to finally come to terms with this, and it's going to shock the hell out of many, but

I'll be living full-time as a female. I intend to make this announcement to the shop very soon."

"That's amazing! Have you talked with a doctor or any other professionals about this?"

"Yes, as a matter of fact I have. I'll be getting new ID that not only includes a name change but will reflect the gender change too. And I intend to have corrective surgery. That's one of the requirements, to see a professional for a certain period of time."

"Wow. You're right about one thing; it will shock some. But hey, if that's what makes you happy and Brenda is good with it, I'm all for you."

"Thank you, sweetie. I love you so much!"

I was overwhelmed that Nicole took it so well. Even though she didn't grow up in my home, in the short time I'd known her as an adult, I'd found her to be very level-headed and understanding. I wanted to tell Michelle too, but the time just wasn't right. She belonged to a very conservative church and I was afraid she'd reject me. I wanted to wait for a better time, a better moment.

I still hadn't told the Women Entrepreneurs of Oregon. Although I'm sure that a few suspected it, I never really said anything to any of them regarding my gender dysphoria and plans to become a full-time woman. After all, it was only January when I'd told Tia I wouldn't be going any further than a feminized male. Of course, back then I didn't realize the urgency of making a definitive decision.

When I realized that living in-between wasn't working, I had to choose a world in which to live, and I'd chosen to be authentic. So on the evening of our monthly WEO meeting, I made my announcement. I decided to go all out with my clothes and wore a sexy, low-cut, sleeveless, pink dress that kind of overwhelmed me at first. I was so used to looking in-between that it took me a bit longer to become comfortable wearing sexy clothes in public. But that was the dress for my announcement.

As usual, Brenda and I arrived a little early to help set up the rented banquet room for the meeting. Although we were long-term members, people took second looks from the moment we entered. Brenda assured me that I was looking great and the girls were just admiring my dress.

Because she had been a member longer than I, Brenda was more comfortable mingling with the others. But on that exciting evening, I got attention as well. Member after member made a point of coming up to me to compliment me on my dress, and I loved it.

Overall, the meetings were structured and included dinner, a speaker, and at the end, a time for announcements and mingling. We always tried to find speakers who were prominent in their fields, well known, and of course, could excite some hard-working, giddy female business owners.

When the speaker had finished and the floor opened for announcements, I started to sweat. The microphone was going around to each table, and at any moment, they would hand it to me.

"Brenda, I'm really nervous," I said.

"Don't be silly, Caisie," she said. "You couldn't be among a more understanding and friendly group. And besides, they all love you!"

I had prepared a statement that I meant to read aloud:

"I have an announcement to make this evening that is somewhat difficult for me. Most of you here tonight remember when I joined Brenda as a member a few years ago and I began attending meetings with her on a regular basis. At that time, I introduced myself as Bill Casey and, for the most part, wore male clothes and conducted myself in that manner. For those of you who were here and remember those days, you also will remember the subtle changes I began to undergo over time—the androgynous clothing, and eventually the makeup. And never once did any of you complain. Well, of course, I was changing, and to be honest, it took me a great deal of time to realize just what was going on. Which brings me to this evening's announcement: I am a transgender female, and I am in the process of changing my ID, including my gender marker. My new name is Caisie Breen Casey—Caisie Breen, for short. I hope this won't change anything between us and…"

That was what I was planning to say.

But when I took the mic and stood up, I simply said, "Hello, ladies. I'm nervous as I can be, so please be nice. I have finally decided to become my authentic self and am in the process of transitioning to female. My new legal name will be Caisie Breen. Thank you all for your patience and support."

At that, everyone began clapping so loudly that I had to sit down and cry tears of joy. I couldn't have asked for a more enthusiastic nod of support. Clearly, they all did love me, and of course, I loved them too. One of the newer members, Monica, a successful young brunette, came up to me and said, "Wow, Caisie. I never would have dreamed that you weren't a naturally born woman. You're gorgeous!" Which, of course, made my joy even greater.

The women of WEO had taught me that there was so much more to being a woman than just sexy clothes and makeup. Indeed, during the years that Brenda and I had been there, I had seen many women come and go, and some of the most beautiful wore simple pantsuits with no makeup at all. The thing I found most attractive was their smile and the way they treated other people. My own Brenda Sweet and Tia fit that description well. They both were beautiful no matter what they wore, and people were attracted to them because they were sincere and caring people. I felt so blessed to have been a member.

Chapter Seventeen

It was time for our September PSI contractors' meeting in Orlando. I packed far more than I had for any previous event. I was torn as to whether or not I would come out and attend in my female wardrobe or hold off until another time, so I packed both men's and women's clothing.

Men's clothing:

  2 pairs pants
  3 t-shirts
  3 shirts
  5 pairs boxer shorts
  5 pairs socks

Women's clothing:

  3 tops
  3 skirts
  3 dresses
  3 bras
  6 pairs panties
  3 pairs knee-hi hose
  3 pairs socks
  2 scarves
  2 pairs flats
  1 pair walking shoes
  2 necklaces
  6 pairs earrings

Complete makeup kit

I went to the airport in my androgynous clothing, and we stood in a very long line waiting to go through the security check. We had our tickets and ID out, and Brenda went through in seconds. When I approached, the agent looked at my ID, then at my face, then back to my ID, and back to my face before finally saying, "Go ahead." I looked exactly like what I was: a middle-aged, short-haired woman with male identification. I couldn't wait for my surgery in four more months so I could change my license and never have to deal with this again.

Once we were through security, Brenda and I sat down for lunch, and I asked, "Did you see how that TSA agent looked at my ID?"

"I did. I was afraid you were going to be pulled aside. He definitely did a double-take."

"I know. My heart dropped when he looked at my ID the third time. So glad I got through without a scene."

When we arrived in Florida later that evening, I decided that it was now or never. I was so close to getting my new ID and going public full-time; to come out right there and then would make our next Expo that much easier. I felt that if I could tell a group of over two thousand construction contractors, I could indeed tell anybody.

I put on my makeup and pantsuit and stepped into the hallway with great trepidation. We made our way to the ballrooms and got in line to register for the event. Because we had been members for so many years, there were many stares.

When we reached our table to sign in, I noticed Patty, one of the event leaders. She looked up at me and simply smiled.

"Hi, Patty," I said, extending my hand. I was so touched. She had to have put things together in a split second, as she knew me well.

After she signed us in, I asked if I could talk to her for a moment in private. She found us a room nearby and led me and Brenda inside.

"Okay, Patty, I'm sure you're probably confused, or at least full of questions. I would be too if I saw a male member whom I'd known for years suddenly show up at a meeting dressed as a woman. But for Brenda and me, this has not been sudden. A few years ago, I discovered that I was transgender—born with a male body but a female brain. Without going into everything, I'll just say it has been one hell of a struggle, but with Brenda's help and full support, I've decided to come out as my authentic self and begin living my true gender. I'm undergoing a legal name change—my new name is Caisie Breen Casey, but I'll be going by Caisie Breen."

Patty put her hand on my forearm and said, "I think it's great that you can be yourself now. And bless you, Brenda, for being there for her. Don't worry about a thing, Caisie. I'll get your new name badges made up at once and make all the changes needed on our documentation. Congratulations, and welcome to the sisterhood."

Brenda looked at me and smiled, then took Patty's hand. "Thank you so much, Patty. Caisie and I both appreciate you and how you're handling all this."

"Hey, that's what I'm here for. Glad to help," Patty replied.

I was surprised at how quickly Patty accepted me. I did wonder if she knew something in advance, although it didn't matter. She was so nice—so gracious.

We went out to find a good place for dinner, and for the most part, I chose to keep a low profile until I saw how well others accepted the new me. Laying low was easy; I already felt like a withering pink carnation in a field of healthy, overgrown ragweeds. From the looks I was getting, many couldn't believe what they were witnessing.

As we waited for our order, I asked, "Okay, sweetie. How am I doing? Patty was great, but have you seen all the looks I'm getting?"

"Oh, honey. Relax. You're doing just fine. Those looks you're getting are mixed. Some have no idea who you were and are simply checking out a foxy lady. And the others? I mean, what would you expect? If you saw one of your friends whom you knew for years and years show up at one of these meetings dressed as a woman, wouldn't you do a double-take?"

"Of course, you're right," I said. "Now that you put it that way, I guess I should feel better that no one has said anything directly to me yet."

The next day we met in the main ballroom for our general meeting with over two thousand macho contractors. It felt like every eye in the place was on me. Every time someone twisted in his or her seat to look in my direction, I felt like a freak on public display. I'm sure the speakers must have wondered what everyone was looking at. I cringed and felt myself sliding lower in my chair. I wanted to crawl under a piece of paper that had fallen on the floor and hide.

After two hours, we had a twenty-minute break. I whispered to Brenda, "Now this can really get interesting."

Everyone filed out to find snacks and chat. As I watched the group leave the ballroom, I noticed an old friend and went up to talk to him. He was about two inches taller than me, with a heavy frame and short brown hair, and it looked like he hadn't shaved in a couple of days. He was facing me, but in a conversation with someone else. I waited for him to finish, and as I reached out my hand to shake his, his eyes got big and he turned his back to me.

That marked the first exchange I'd had, good or bad, with any of the other contractors. But we still had the last event, vendors' night, to attend. Vendors were given floor space in a large ballroom to display their products.

I decided to wear my more modest, pink-and-black business dress. I did my makeup a little louder than usual, as I knew the evening lights would be low. I didn't want to look too sultry. As we entered the hallway, Brenda took my arm, and we proceeded toward the ballroom.

As always, the room was so packed. As Brenda and I began to visit the vendor booths, she whispered, "Do you hear that? That drunk is following you and is yelling something at us."

I have a partial hearing loss and couldn't hear him. I looked behind me and saw a drunken contractor tipping back a beer and glaring at me. I had never in my adult life feared for my safety, but I was afraid of this large, gruff, cowboy-looking man.

"He's just drunk," I said. "It'll be fine." But as we went on, he became louder and louder. Nobody in the ballroom said anything to him, nor did they make any efforts to stop him. In fairness to the organizers, there was so much noise that they probably didn't notice.

"Let's get the hell out of here!" I said. We quickly found our way back to our room and decided to stay there for the rest of the evening. "Wow. That was one crazy son of a bitch!"

"I know. And it took you forever to hear him," Brenda replied.

"Did you understand what he was yelling?"

"No. There was too much noise. But he definitely had a problem with you. And the more we ignored him, the louder he got."

Well, we go home tomorrow. I know I lost one friend for sure. I couldn't believe he did that—turned and put his back right up in my face, when I tried to shake his hand. Amazing!"

"I know. That really shocked me too. I'm afraid there are a lot of members who're just going to need some time. But who knows; maybe next time things will be better."

"Yeah. You're right. I hope so."

I then began to think about the drunk again, and how I was unable to protect Brenda.

"You know, Brenda; when that drunk came after us, I was just as helpless and scared as you. I guess that's one thing I hadn't thought of when I began my 'softer me' change. And I have to tell you, I have a whole new appreciation of what most women have to put up with on a daily basis. Again, I don't have the same body strength I used to, and I fell short when it came time to protect you. That's not gonna change. Are you okay with that?"

"Oh, you. Don't be silly! For one thing, where is it written the male must always be 'the protector' of the female? And two, even when you were all buff and strong, there was always someone stronger. So c'mon, honey. You have nothing to feel bad about. And yes; most women do feel vulnerable around men they don't know, especially in unfamiliar settings. But hey, we did the right thing by leaving the room, and we're gonna be fine."

Back home, I decided it was time to tell my employees but I wanted to check with Brenda first.

"Hey, Brenda Sweet. I'm planning on making my announcement to the shop in a few days. Are you okay with that?"

"That seems kind of sudden. I want to see a therapist first, and besides, I thought you wanted to have new ID before you told the office staff."

I did, and I'm sorry. I didn't know you wanted to see a therapist. Anyway, two of our plumbers, Theo and Darin, found out about me from a customer who saw me on

Facebook, so you know it's only a matter of time before everyone knows."

"Oh, I didn't know that. Well, you're exactly right. If you're going to control the message, you have to move on it. Make your announcement. I'm still making an appointment to see a therapist, but yes—do it."

I met privately with both of my plumbers the next day in my office.

"Hi, Theo and Darin. Thanks for coming in. Go ahead and shut the door and have a seat. So, I understand you've heard some news about me from a customer?" I said.

They both were visibly nervous as they walked in. They looked at each other with wide eyes, then back at me as they took their seats.

"Well, yeah. And I think it's fine. You won't have any issues from me," said Darin, as he did a little seat squirming.

"Thank you so much, Darin. That means so much to me. And just what exactly is it that you heard? What is it that you are so graciously willing to support?"

"Well, you know—you becoming a woman. And again, no problem!" he said.

"And you, Theo?" I asked.

"I'm with Darin. No problem. It takes guts to do what you're doing. I'll support you."

"I'm very touched, you guys. I'd appreciate it if you'd do a little Internet research on your own regarding gender dysphoria. It will give you a better picture of where I'm at and how I got here. I'll be announcing this soon to the whole shop, but until then, please don't say anything."

They assured me they wouldn't say a word. I decided I would make my announcement from home, via speakerphone, the following Tuesday during their safety meeting.

"Hello. Can everyone hear me?" I said.

I could almost see them looking back and forth at each other as they answered, "Oh yeah, sure, yes, we hear you fine."

"What I'm about to tell you may rock your boat, unless you've already heard the rumors. After struggling for years with gender dysphoria, I have recently thrown in the towel and have decided to begin living authentically as a female. If you had no idea that this was coming, I certainly understand how this would be a shock to you. But for Brenda and me, this is something that gradually began revealing itself many years ago, and I simply suppressed it. After much discussion with professionals, we decided that coming out as my true brain gender was my best course of action. Because I don't want to cause any discomfort at the shop, I won't be coming in anymore. I will be working remotely from home from now on. Any questions?"

To a person, everyone supported me and told me not to worry about anything. I found myself weeping and had to hang up quickly. Their warm, supportive response was more than I could have hoped for. Still, I wasn't convinced that they would be comfortable with my presence. I think it was probably more me than them, but I chose to let things settle in for as long as it took before I came back to the shop.

The only people who didn't know about my changes yet were Michelle, my mother, my three brothers, my older sister, and my neighbors. I had no interest in telling my mother at that time or one of my two younger brothers, Bret, as we weren't speaking. It had been so long since we spoke that I didn't even remember what the original problem was.

I called Valerie and told her my story. She didn't receive the news well at all.

"Hello, Valerie. How have you been?"

"Good. I see you on Facebook a lot lately. Is that really you?"

"Ah, well, what do you mean, 'Is that really you?'"

"Oh, c'mon, Bill. Who are you trying to kid? Putting yourself out there as a middle-aged woman for all the world to see. Geez, aren't you embarrassed?"

"Val, I'm a transgender woman. I've finally come to grips with something that's been tearing me apart for years."

"No, you're not! You should be ashamed of yourself. You're an embarrassment..."

And she continued on with her rant, so cold and heartless that I hung up and ran to my bedroom bawling.

"What's wrong, Caisie? My goodness, what happened?" Brenda asked.

I finally composed myself enough to blubber, "My sister said mean things about me and was horribly vicious when I told her."

Brenda took me in her arms and said, "Oh, sweetie, I'm so sorry. We won't need to talk to her anymore."

We still haven't.

The next morning, I called my youngest brother Corey, who was surprisingly supportive. After Valerie, I guess I didn't know what to expect from the rest of them—Corey, Steve, and Bret. Corey's biggest problem was getting used to calling me by my new name. That I could deal with, as we rarely saw each other anyway.

I then decided to call my older brother, Steve. He lived in another state, and even though we had grown up in different households, I'd always felt a close bond with him. I thought if anyone would understand, he would.

"Hi, Steve," I said when I called him. "I see you've been following me on Facebook. So, you know I'm transgender, right?" I had before-and-after pictures there along with posts about my transition.

"Have you seen a professional?" he asked.

"As a matter of fact, I have."

"Good. Because I think that's what's needed here, Bill."

Bill? I thought. My new name was all over my Facebook page. *Bill? Really?*

"Okay, Steve. Thanks for being understanding. I gotta go. Later," I said, and hung up.

After our conversation, Steve posted on my Facebook page, "You need a doc, bro. There's something wrong with you. You need help."

It was one thing to dismiss me as a kook, but to publicly humiliate me was more than I was ready for. I was brokenhearted and unsure of what to do or how to do it. So, like every other time in my life when I had come face to face with such turmoil, I turned to the one thing I could always rely on: music.

I immediately sought out songs that would bring me some relief and peace. I came across a powerful YouTube video of "Songbird" by Christine McVie of Fleetwood Mac.

I reposted it on my Facebook page.

> *For you, there'll be no more crying. For you,*
> *the sun will be shining…*

> *And the songbirds are singing, like they know the score.*
> *And I love you, I love you, I love you, like never before…*
> *And I wish you all the love in the world.*
> *But most of all, I wish it from myself.*

The song was perfect. I desperately needed to hear those words: *"For you, there'll be no more crying. For you, the sun will be shining…"*

It occurred to me that there were many other birds just like me. Birds who go through life-changing events facing ridicule, resentment, and all too often, outright rejection. So often we get hurt by those we thought loved us unconditionally.

We *do* know the score. I had found a place of refuge right there on Facebook among my like-minded friends.

From that day on, I personalized the word by spelling it "songbyrd." It became the name I used for my many friends who also lived and breathed music.

After I posted that song on my Facebook page, my friend Xenia from Wales quickly and unexpectedly came to my defense and brought me enough strength to deal with my brother. She was another sister and one of my first trans Facebook friends. As a fellow songbyrd, she knew right away that I was deeply hurt. So as any good friend would, she posted a Beatles song on my timeline, along with a very simple, sweet message which read… "Hey Caisie. Hang in there GF. Here's a song just for you."

That made me cry even harder, but her kind actions also gave me the strength to do something positive for myself. It was hard, but I blocked Steve on Facebook and in effect severed my relationship with the same big brother who protected me from bullies when I was a little child, and whom I thought loved me as much as I did him. Clearly, I was wrong. I knew there would be some casualties when I came out, but never dreamed he would be one of them. And thank God for precious friends like Xenia, who were sensitive enough to notice when a friend was hurt and kind enough to do something about it. Who knows how long I might have floundered about in uncertainty had she not gotten involved.

CHAPTER EIGHTEEN

Because I had told almost everyone I was transgender, I was even more anxious to have my orchi and get my new ID. Although I would have preferred the complete sex reassignment surgery—SRS for short—I decided to get the minimum done because of the huge expense. But getting the "minimum" done was something that was by no means easy or pleasant.

And then there was sex. *How's this going to work?* I thought. *Brenda has never been sexually attracted to women. What are we going to do?* It was plain to see that after thirty years of marriage, having sex as "man and wife" was no longer an option.

"Tomorrow's your big day," Brenda said.

"Yeah, I'm really looking forward to it. How about you, honey? You've been so supportive. How are you feeling?"

"Oh, I'm fine, I guess. I mean, of course I'm missing my husband, and my therapist says that's normal. There's going to be a mourning process. But I'm fine, and I'll adjust. I won't be happy, really, unless you are, but yes, I'm finding that I need time. I've never been here before, but as long as you're here, it's going to be fine."

Brenda saw her therapist just after I made my announcement to my shop, and after a few visits, I joined her. And my eyes were opened. It's not unusual for those of us in transition to get so caught up in our euphoria of becoming authentic that we fail to recognize the total impact on others. Indeed, there is a death, and there is a mourning process that will occur. My Brenda Sweet, yes, she supported my change, but she had loved and been married to Bill Casey for thirty years. He just died.

"Oh, honey. I feel so selfish. All this time, I've been so focused on my changes and adjustments. I feel like I've totally ignored and overlooked everyone else! I'm so sorry. And sweetie, I have to ask you. Are you going to be able to adjust to not having a man in bed?"

"Oh, you. Of course! We've been getting by and always seem to find ways to satisfy each other. Thanks for being sensitive, but really, I'll be fine."

We embraced each other, knowing we were in uncharted waters but confident we'd help each other make it through.

I arrived as scheduled on January 20, 2012, to have my surgery. We pulled into the driveway of a single-story house that had been converted into a medical office. The waiting room was a former living room with four wooden chairs against the wall. I signed in with the front desk and was told I'd be taken back to the room where my procedure would be performed, while Brenda waited out front.

I followed the receptionist down a narrow hallway, and she asked me to enter the medical room and wait for the doctor. I was overwhelmed by a powerful smell of rubbing alcohol. It was a typical clinical procedure room—brown, padded examination table, a single chair, and cabinets. I jumped up and sat on the table and began to do some reflecting while I waited for my doctor. I didn't have the fifteen thousand dollars for surgery and had to put it on my credit card. But at least I'd be able to get the gender marker on my ID corrected.

The doctor came in with a male assistant. He was a short, slim man in his fifties, and his assistant was a curly-haired, stocky man who stood at least six inches taller than the doctor.

"Hello, Caisie Breen. I'm Dr. Lyle. How are you today?"

"I'm fine, Doctor," I said.

"Wonderful. Well, this is your big day. Are you ready to go through with it?"

"Oh, yes. I'm so ready," I replied.

"All right, I have to have a male assistant now. After this procedure, if you decide to have the full SRS, we'll need a woman, as you'll then legally be female. Okay, I need you to just lie back. I'm going to give you a few locals. There's no need to knock you out for this procedure. Do you have any questions?"

"No. I'm ready," I said.

He injected an anesthetic beneath my scrotum and left for about fifteen minutes to give the injections time to work. My equipment had never been very generous, and since I'd been on hormones, my testes had retracted inside. I couldn't help wonder how that was going to work. I mean, he'd administered the injections way down below.

The doctor returned and made a small nick with a scalpel. "Did you feel that?"

"No, didn't feel a thing. We're good," I replied.

He made a much wider opening and began inserting what looked like a pair of surgical pliers inside me. All of a sudden, I felt the blood drain from my face. I desperately needed some air.

"Are you okay, Caisie?"

"I'll be fine, but I've got to have some air. Please open the door," I replied. So his surgical assistant opened the door, and what a relief it was. That was the good news. The bad news? Everyone in the waiting room was about to hear the rest of my procedure.

The doctor began to probe higher, looking for a testis as I lay there with my jaw clenched in pain, trying hard not to say anything.

"Caisie, are you going to be okay? I still can't find what I'm looking for, and I don't want to hurt you," said Dr. Lyle.

"Don't worry about me, Doctor. You can't stop; you've got to complete the procedure."

He went up a little farther and said, "There's one!" He grabbed it with his pliers and began pulling it down far enough to cut it off. No longer able to remain quiet, I let out one of the saddest, most horrifying screams, which echoed out into the hallway and on down into the waiting room.

Startled, Dr. Lyle said, "Caisie, I think we need to stop. I don't want to hurt you."

In tears, with sweat pouring, I begged him, with clenched jaw, "Please, no. I can do this. Don't listen to me! I'm going to scream, but I'll be okay. Please, I must have this procedure. I can't get my new ID without it. Please don't stop."

He reluctantly proceeded. I did get through the torture. After that, he sewed me up and Ms. Caisie Breen walked out of that procedure room. On the way out, I couldn't help but notice all the watery eyes, especially Brenda's. It was difficult to walk, but the relief of having it over with made my heart soar. Brenda helped me to our car, and we went home a new couple, indeed!

The day after my procedure, I walked like a rodeo cowboy, but my Brenda Sweet knew how to take away the pain. When I walked into our bedroom that evening, she had made a gorgeous, colorful banner that read, "CAISIE BREEN I LOVE U."

"You crazy, gorgeous woman, you! Come here," I said. I gave her a kiss that couldn't begin to express all the love I felt for her.

Three days later, I went to the courthouse and got my court-ordered name change, complete with new gender marker. With that, I was able to get a new social security card and even a new birth certificate. The hardest thing to change, surprisingly, was my utility bill. I was able to do everything else through the mail, but my electric company needed a face-to-face. I also had to do my driver's license in person. And it was interesting.

"Hello. I'm here to get a new driver's license," I said to a woman at a glass window.

"You'll need to take a number and wait over there. After your number is called, you'll get your picture taken, then come back over here and you'll get your new driver's license," she replied.

"Cool." I then got a number and sat down.

"Number 9?"

"That's me."

"Sit right over there, to the right a little—there." Flash!

"Is that it?" I asked the cameraman.

"That's it," he replied.

Excited then, I hustled back up to the counter and stood in line. When my turn came, the lady who had waited on me earlier got my new license, complete with my new picture, handed it to me, and asked me to check it for accuracy.

"Oh, no. What an awful picture," I said.

"Oh, well. Nobody likes their picture. But how about the text, the information. Is it accurate?"

Even with my glasses, I need to use a magnifying glass for small print and my driver's license was small print. I squinted and scanned it, looking for the gender marker. *The 'M' better be replaced with an "F,"* I thought. It was a good thing I checked, because they forgot to make that critical change.

"Ah, miss. There's a mistake here. The gender marker has an 'M.' We need to change that to an 'F.'"

"Oh, no. I don't know how I missed that! Of course. I'll just be a few more minutes. I'll do another one."

Once the correction was made, I left as one very happy new Oregon driver.

I still hadn't told my mother or my neighbors, and although Nicole had told Michelle, I hadn't talked with her yet. I was still terrified I'd lose her. I knew my mother wouldn't understand, as we hadn't talked in years. So I just sent her a copy of my new birth certificate along with a short note that explained everything about my new identity and being transgender. She never responded.

I had lived in the same neighborhood for over thirty years and knew most of my neighbors well enough to call them by their first names. I decided to discuss how to approach each of them with Brenda.

"Hey, honey. What do you think I should do with our neighbors? I'm sure that most of them are going to think I'm a raging hypocrite. All the times I was at their door gathering signatures for anti-gay petitions and now, "Oh, by the way, I'm a trans female."

"Well, I'm afraid I have to agree a little. There's going to be some fallout. I hope nobody eggs our house. I think to be safe, I would just send letters to those we've known the longest," said Brenda.

I sent them all a letter of explanation at the same time I sent my mother her note. And half of them did turn their backs on me. I certainly couldn't hold that against them. For the most part, I kept to myself at home.

CHAPTER NINETEEN

Two weeks after my orchi and name change, I woke up early to "Hey Jude" playing on my sound system. Brenda took me to the hospital, where I was to have an angioplasty performed. My angina was back, along with a debilitating pain. During a recent treadmill stress test at the hospital, I lasted only six seconds when they began to incline the machine.

I felt fortunate that I was being treated under my new name. I had waited so long and been through so much to finally live an authentic life. But after living fifty-five years as a male, most of it under the same medical plan, I couldn't help but wonder if my medical care would be different. Had they ever treated openly transgender patients before, and were they prepared to deal with me? It wasn't so long ago that I was a narrow-minded bigot and thought that gays and transgender people should just stop living that way. Would I run into any doctors with similar views?

I was on a gurney, being wheeled down an incredibly long hallway, headed to an operating room. They were going to send a tiny camera down my artery as a part of performing the angioplasty or placing a stent. They'd made it clear that there was no guarantee that it would work, and that if the artery was too clogged, they would have to immediately perform emergency open-heart surgery.

The sterile smells of antiseptic lingered in the air, and the room was freezing. The doctor gave me a sedative and anesthetic to numb the area where they would be inserting the camera. I fell into what seemed like a brief, thirty-second sleep. When I woke up, my doctor began to talk to me.

"Caisie, you're a very lucky woman. Your primary artery entering the heart was 85 percent blocked. We call that a widow maker. If you'd had a heart attack in this condition, you wouldn't have survived. They're preparing the surgery room for you now." He paused. "We've explained all of this to Brenda, and she'll be there for you when we're done. Do you have any questions before we begin?"

I don't know which comment brought the most emotion: "You're a very lucky woman," or "If you'd had a heart attack in this condition, you wouldn't have survived." It was so satisfying to hear my new gender being honored, but being told I might not have survived dampened the joy.

"No, Doctor. I'm ready," I replied.

"Great. I need to get to surgery and prepare things for you. Tim, your anesthesiologist, will take over now and make sure you get delivered in one piece," said Doctor Shely. He winked. Tim told me that I probably would be "going out" while en route to surgery and asked me if there was anything I wanted to say before that happened.

"Yes, as a matter of fact. I know this may sound silly, but I know that while I'm out, you'll probably have a bunch of hoses down my throat. I think I would be terrified if they were still in place when I came to."

The anesthesiologist replied with a slight laugh, "Okay, no problem. I'll see what I can do."

With that, we began the long ride down the hallway to surgery. Seconds later, I was out.

Again, I felt as if I'd only been asleep for thirty seconds. I couldn't talk; somebody was trying desperately to retrieve the hoses from my throat before I regained full consciousness.

"Hi, Caisie. How are you feeling? You've just come out of surgery and everything went well," the anesthesiologist said.

My tongue was so dry it stuck to the roof of my mouth. "I'm fine, but I think I'm still drunk."

He laughed and said, "Someone will be in shortly to take you to your room. I'm going out now to tell Brenda so she can meet you there."

It's a cliché, but I felt like I'd seen my life flash before my eyes, so realistic it seemed like a 3-D movie. I remembered so many minute details, which was amazing, as my memory had always been terrible. There was something else, too. Something inside had changed, although at that moment I had no idea what it was. The only word I could think of was *supernatural*.

I was delighted to see Brenda waiting in the recovery room with a colorful bouquet of flowers. "Hi, honey. How are you feeling?" she asked as the gurney driver put my bed in place.

"Not feeling any pain, at least not yet. Any idea how long I'm going to have to stay here?" I asked.

"Whoa, now slow down, honey," Brenda said. "You've just had major open-heart surgery. It's not like your orchi, where you can just get up and go home. The doctor will be in soon. I'm sure he'll have some instructions for you."

She was absolutely right, of course. The only reason I felt as good as I did was because I was on strong painkillers. I had small tubes in my arms and a couple of large ones that went up into my rib cage.

After about an hour, the attending physician came in to explain everything. "Ms. Breen, the surgery went very well, and we expect you to make a full recovery. You're very fortunate to have come in when you did. You'll probably be here at least a week in recovery, and you'll be doing some special exercises every day. Any questions?"

"No. I think you've spelled it out pretty well. Thanks for saving my life," I said.

"No need to thank me. It was a team effort. You just do your exercises and get out of here, okay?"

"Sounds like a plan, Doctor," I said.

I began my required walking exercises the next day. The goal was to walk completely around the ward without stopping. With Brenda by my side, I made it about a fourth of the way.

Three days later, I found out how well my heart was being monitored. In the wee hours of the morning, I noticed some scruff on my face and felt a sudden and desperate need to shave it off. So I grabbed the pole holding the hoses I was attached to and walked into the bathroom to shave. Just as I made the first stroke with my razor, I heard something that sounded like a person blowing through tightened lips and making a small motor sound. Then I felt it. My heart rate had shot up so fast I couldn't count the beats. It felt weird, but it didn't hurt, so I continued to shave.

The emergency team flew into the room in surgical gowns, caps, and masks. They looked at me in astonishment. One of them said, "Caisie, what are you doing up? Get back in bed at once!"

"Okay, okay, Doctor, I'm almost…"

"Now, Caisie! Don't you hear that alarm? This is serious business!"

With that, I dropped my razor and climbed back into bed with my half-shaven face against the pillow so no one would notice. After a few tests, they determined everything was fine, and shortly thereafter, my heartbeat returned to normal. The doctor later told me that what occurred wasn't too unusual, and that no damage had been done.

I continued to exercise with Brenda by my side and was eventually able to walk around the entire ward. That allowed me to return home. But I wasn't the same person. Something had changed.

After I'd been home for about a week, one of the changes became terribly and wonderfully clear. My senses were off the charts. I felt happiness like I'd never experienced before, and pain —well let's just say I didn't handle emotional pain well at all. I cried at almost anything: a sad news story involving an injured kitty, a happy story of a young soldier coming home from service early and surprising his wife. But the change I enjoyed the most was my re-energized interest in music. I started to pick up on different genres and different artists I'd never listened to or even liked before. Artists like Metallica, Aerosmith, and Pink Floyd, to name a few. I couldn't get enough of those guys. As time went on, I became almost insatiable. I began to dig deeper and farther back and looked for more artists and songs I might have missed in my early years. If my thirst for music was a ten before, it was one hundred and ten after my heart surgery. It was almost like I could hear it in in 3-D, but it was more than that.

After my little shaving experience in the hospital, I decided to look to permanent facial hair removal with electrolysis. Brenda directed me to a woman who'd done the same procedure for her.

"Hi," I said when I met her. "I'm Caisie. As you can see, I have a little scruff on my face I'd like to have removed."

"Oh, hi, Caisie. I'm Barbara. It looks like you don't actually have much hair to deal with."

"Yeah, I've never had much facial or body hair. I don't even have to shave my legs. From my knees down, I'm as smooth as a baby's butt."

"I wonder...you told me on the phone that you're in transition, male to female?"

"Yes."

"I wonder if you have the double X chromosome."

Her comment caused me to do a little thinking. *Hmm, is there a medical explanation for all this, for me?*

Much of Barbara's clientele was from the transgender community, so she wasn't afraid of intimate conversation. Even though I had just met her, I felt like I had known her for much longer, and her questions didn't bother me a bit.

Although I had very little hair, I did have to continue regular treatments for over six months before I could switch from shaving with a razor to using tweezers for an occasional weeding. And though the treatments were painful, I always looked forward to the conversations with Barbara. Every time I visited, she managed to work "I can't believe how little hair you have" into the conversation.

Now that I was living full-time as a woman, I made every effort to keep my promise not to go to the office. As the founder and owner, however, it was becoming harder and harder for me to stay away. Everyone, even Nicole, accepted the new me, so I decided I'd spoken too quickly and just showed up one afternoon. There was just one problem: Michelle came in on a regular basis to clean our offices. She and I still hadn't spoken much.

I pulled into the driveway and saw her car and my two young grandsons, Corban and Zander, playing around back. Michelle was loading her cleaning buckets. When she saw me, she seemed unsure about what to do. She walked to my car window, looked at me with kind of a half-smile, and said hello. And because that was the first time she saw me as Caisie Breen, I started my car and left. I knew she was still digesting things, and I didn't want to cause her any unnecessary discomfort. Michelle and I did message each other occasionally on Facebook, but it was clear she was going to need some time. It felt like she was trying to avoid me. Before my change, I saw her at the shop quite often. After my announcement, I didn't see her again until this one occasion. Other than accidentally bumping into her at the office, it didn't look like we were going to have a relationship again anytime soon. After a few weeks, she stopped coming to our shop completely to clean the offices. It hurt, but I had to move on and simply give her whatever time she needed. I was at a total loss. I didn't know what to say, or if there was anything I could say that would make us close again.

CHAPTER TWENTY

I was finally out full-time and was determined to have some summer fun. But I first wanted to work on some of my mannerisms, particularly my voice.

"Hey, Brenda Sweet. What do you think of my voice? I've been trying to get my pitch up a little higher, but it's hard," I said.

"It's going to take some practice, honey. You've got over fifty years of talking with a male voice to overcome. But you don't really need to come up very much. Just practice."

"Yeah, you're right. And I've seen voice coaches on the Net. I think I'm going to check some of them out."

"Sure. That should help speed things along."

The one that attracted me most was exceptionalvoice.com, a website by voice instructor Kathe Perez. I called to inquire about her voice classes, and she gave me a quick sample.

"Okay, Caisie. Say the word 'up.' You'll feel the larynx hop slightly. Keep repeating 'up,' raising the pitch slightly each time. If you have a piano, follow a scale. After a few iterations, you won't be able to go any higher. This is the limit of your natural voice. But don't worry, we can change it! Keep going upward and you'll feel a strange *crack* in your larynx; this is the falsetto range. You'll sound like a cartoon character, but that doesn't matter. We'll use this as a base for building your new voice.

Begin working your way downward, speaking/singing all the while. You'll want to get to the divide between your natural voice and your falsetto. If you do it right, you should cross the gap and have a high voice that sounds somewhat natural. Keep talking; it helps you concentrate on the new voice. Read a poem or a book out loud if you're not good at stream-of-consciousness. Do this for a few minutes, until you feel uncomfortable holding your voice up there. Get a drink of water... And don't forget, practice, practice, practice, practice!"

"Wow, Kathe. That was a lot of information."

"No worries, Caisie. That was just a quick overview to give you something to work on after we hang up. During our sessions, we'll be working at your pace, okay? Sound like something you want to try?"

"Sure," I said. "Let's give it a go."

I spent three weeks working with her before I finally gave up. I felt that I just wasn't getting it, and even though we could see each other via Skype, it just didn't feel personal enough. So I sought out a local voice coach. I was surprised to find a woman who not only lived nearby, but was very trans friendly. All her clients were male to female.

In-person coaching was much better for me, and I made progress right away. I continued with her for two months until I felt I was speaking in a good voice range for a female. The sad thing was that, because I didn't keep up my practice, I went back to my old voice in less than a year. I did remember the basics, though, and could go to my feminine voice at will.

It was August 2012, a great time to test some of my new feminine skills in public. Brenda and I decided to attend a popular event called Bite of Oregon in downtown Portland. There would be a multitude of food booths from local chefs, as well as wine-tasting.

"Hey, Sweet. What do you think of this? It's light and breezy," I asked, holding up a pretty pink-and-black spring dress.

"Oh, yes," she answered. "That's perfect for today. And here, here's a summer hat that will set things off really well."

I was a little nervous. It had been a year since I'd worn a dress in public, and that was in Seattle. But Seattle was fantastic, and I did look pretty good in that slinky little spring dress. And with my makeup and hat, I had to admit I looked beautiful.

"What do you think, Brenda Sweet?"

"Wow. You're really doing great. Your makeup is flawless, you couldn't have picked out a better dress, and I love how cute the hat looks on you," she said.

Everything went smoothly until we bought food and walked to a table. I was startled when a gust of wind shot up my dress and made me feel like I was standing half-naked in public for a moment.

"Woo-hoo! Little side show, honey?" Brenda laughed.

With an alarmed smile, I snapped my arm down against the fluttering dress and saved myself some of the embarrassment in time. But, wow! That's what women have to put up with and have dealt with for ages.

"So how'd I handle that, hun? I mean, I was focusing on my walk, but when the wind did that to my dress…shit! I felt like everyone was looking right at me—that they were going to laugh," I said.

"Oh, honey," Brenda giggled. "Didn't you see the other women defending their innocence at the same time? You weren't the only woman wearing a dress—and no, no one paid any attention to your little blow-up. I thought you looked cute."

"Ha, okay. Glad you were amused," I said.

We sat and watched people streaming by. Most were middle-aged like us, but there were some in their twenties and thirties. That's probably why there was such a variety of music playing. As we sat there, I heard a song that I couldn't make out. "Brenda," I asked. "What is that song? I know I've heard it before, and I just love it!"

"Seriously? That's "I Was Made For Lovin' You" by KISS. You've always hated KISS. You're saying you like them now?"

"Wow. That's KISS? Well, I don't care who they are. I just love that sound!" I said.

My appetite and appreciation for new music was expanding, and it still surprised me each time I rediscovered a long-forgotten or discarded song or artist. It was as if I had always hated spinach and one day I wasn't able to get enough of it.

After a brief rest, we continued through the display tents and laughed together every time the wind took another swing at my dress. There were no issues of passing whatsoever. Brenda and I both looked beautiful, and my feminine walk was nearly perfect.

There was still a lot of summer left, and Brenda's Aunt Becky did something that touched me to my core. She owned a beach house and put together a weekend sleep over "for the girls," and invited me. Talk about my emotions going sky-high. I cried tears of happiness the moment I received the invitation.

I'd been experimenting in the kitchen and could cook like never before. The other women asked me to make the salad. I felt that every leaf available, any leaf that could be bought, needed to be in my salads.

Brenda and I went to a local farmers' market while the other women went to do some exploring. I was able to find red lettuce, green lettuce, spinach, chard, Frisee, arugula, endive, radicchio, Mizuna, escarole, baby beet greens, cress, Tatsoi, butterhead lettuce, oakleaf, and loose-leaf lettuce. And that was just the greens. I added celery, broccoli, carrots, leeks, and cherry tomatoes. Fortunately, there was a huge five-gallon wooden salad bowl in one of the cupboards, and my salad took up every inch of it. I had gone through so many changes that year, and creativity in the kitchen clearly was among them. Once I saw all my ingredients laid out on the countertop, however, even I thought I might have overdone it. But it was a fantastic salad, and everyone complimented me on my newfound talent.

After the other women returned, we had dinner and then went into the family room where we relaxed, laughed, and chatted. When it came to lively discussions, you could always count on Aunt Becky—someone might be quiet, but she'd have them laughing in no time. We laughed until I was exhausted.

Finally, I said, "Hey, Becky, it's been fun, but we're tired. I think we're going to have to call it a night."

"Oh, yeah? Party pooper. Be that way," Becky said. "See ya in the morning."

We had two relaxing days with Becky and her friends, and I felt a warm camaraderie with my aunt I'd never before experienced. To be welcomed as one of them for a weekend sleepover was more than I ever could have expected. Aunt Becky definitely earned my "heroine of the year" award.

Getting out more often, especially during the summer months after my ID change, boosted my confidence. I had so many new dresses to choose from, and it no longer mattered where I wore them. I was well received everywhere and couldn't wait to do more exploring with Brenda.

Practically everyone on her side of the family had learned of my transition, but not everyone had seen the new me. That changed at the 2012 Fiske family reunion. I was nervous because of my earlier right-wing activism; two of Brenda's cousins were gay.

It would be so easy for them to consider me a hypocrite and perhaps even treat me unkindly. And, frankly, I wouldn't have held it against them. Back when I was naïve and ignorant, I really didn't hate anyone, but until I came face to face with my own reality, I believed that I was dealing with a behavior, not an identity. So when I finally saw my horrific error in 2005, I fell into a state of shame and regret. How could I face them? What could I say? Sorry, I felt, would never be enough, but it was all I had. If they had a problem with me, I would certainly understand.

It was a potluck, and I prepared potato salad, spicy chicken, green bean casserole, and cornbread. When we pulled into the small, secluded park next to the Clackamas River, I spotted an area with a multitude of picnic tables, sheltered from the sun, where many had already arrived and were arranging their food on the tables in preparation for the feast. I grabbed an armload of our food, and as I proceeded to the setup area, I turned around and saw Donna, one of Brenda's gay cousins, walking toward me.

"Hi, Donna," I said, rattled. "Long time no see. Good to see you. Did you have any trouble finding the park?" I didn't know what else to say.

"Oh, hi, Caisie," Donna answered. "No, we've been here before, so it wasn't a problem."

With that, I gave her a quick hug and we both walked toward the noisy group who had already made themselves at home. I breathed an incredible sigh of relief—what an absolute act of grace. I didn't deserve forgiveness, but she extended it anyway. My heart was filled with hope. There was only Doug, Brenda's other gay cousin, left. I prayed a silent prayer that he would find it in his heart to forgive me too.

Aunt Becky announced it was time to eat, and everyone lined up. There was enough food to feed all of us, times three: fried chicken, baked chicken, barbecued chicken, pork ribs, beef ribs, hot dogs, five different styles of potato salads, green salads, rolls, potato chips, and more.

After I ate to full-satiation-plus-one, I got up to walk some of it off. It was such a beautiful area, especially next to the gently flowing river. Near the riverbank, I noticed Doug standing next to a huge willow tree, watching the water as if he had something on his mind.

I walked up to him and with a warm hug said, "I'm so sorry," trying hard not to cry.

He answered "Hey, it's all right, it's all right." We didn't need any long conversations. He knew me well and understood my sorrow instantly. We were at peace with each other again, and everyone on Brenda's side of the family had embraced me in ways I would never have expected. I went back to join the others, grateful that everyone treated me, the new me, Caisie Breen, with love and acceptance.

CHAPTER TWENTY-ONE

"But I'm a creep, I'm a weirdo,
What the hell am I doing here?

I don't belong here, I don't belong here."

"Creep" by Radiohead

As wonderful as it was that I was being accepted by others, I began having some issues of self-acceptance. It was great having a new ID and being able to wear my new clothes and makeup anywhere in public. But every time I went to the bathroom and came face to face with what was left of my old plumbing, I felt freakish and depressed. It was still 2012, just before Thanksgiving, when I began to explore my options.

I contacted the doctor who performed my orchi to see what it would cost to complete my SRS. Because I'd already had the orchi, the rest of the procedure would cost less than I anticipated. But it was something that involved Brenda, so I decided to consult with her that evening, after I got the information from the doctor.

"Hi, honey," I said. "Would you please come in here? I'd like to talk with you if you have time."

"Sure. So what's up?" She turned to face me. "I can tell that something's been bothering you. Let's talk."

I looked into Brenda's eyes and took a deep breath. "You know that I would have preferred to have a complete SRS when I did my orchi, but we didn't have the money. But since then, I've felt so freakish. I know that some trans women get by with this simple change, but frankly, I don't want to think of myself as trans. I'm a woman. But when I go to the bathroom or shower, I'm constantly reminded that my parts are out of whack. I'd really like to complete my SRS." I paused. "What do you think, dear?"

"Oh, honey," Brenda answered. "I knew something was wrong. You haven't played that kind of downer music since you first began struggling with this. Of course, I support you. But you do understand this is a much more serious operation, right?"

"Oh, yes."

"And doctors? Have you found one who can do it?"

"Actually, I was going to have the same one who did my orchi."

"Really? After all the pain you went through?"

"I know, but this time I'll be completely out, and because he did the orchi, the rest of the SRS will be less money."

"Speaking of which; do we have the funds?"

"Yes. I still have some stocks I can cash out that would just cover it."

"Well, go ahead then. Let's do it."

I grabbed her into my arms and said, "Thank you, honey. Oh, I love you so much."

When I went to see Dr. Lyle the following week, he said, "Caisie! Caisie Breen. Good to see you. How have you been? I was so worried about you during your last procedure. I'd never seen anyone with their testes up so high. And I hated going on after I realized how much pain you were in."

"I'm fine, Doctor. Everything's okay. I'd like to schedule the completion of my SRS and a breast augmentation. And I should tell you, I had open heart surgery two weeks after my orchiectomy."

"I'm glad everything's all right, but your heart surgery could be a problem. Unlike your last procedure, we'll have to put you completely out for this one, which will require a cardiac clearance. Please get back to my nurse with something from your cardiologist stating you're fit for surgery, and we'll get you scheduled. We'll want to do the procedures a week apart."

"Okay, Doctor. I'll get right on it," I said.

I got my cardiac clearance and immediately forwarded it to Dr. Lyle, who scheduled my breast augmentation for February 8, and the genital surgery for February 15, 2013. I was absolutely giddy. Finally, a real vagina—a total and complete woman inside and out.

At my pre-op consultation, I was told that the doctor utilized a rented clinic for his surgeries. This wasn't unusual; at the time very few hospitals allowed SRS procedures in their facilities. For my breast implants, I would be in and out in a few hours. The following week, I was told to arrive at 6 a.m. for my SRS and that I would have a three-day recovery at home. On the fourth day, the doctor would make a house call to remove the packing and instruct me on dilating. I needed to insert expansion stents several times a day to keep my vagina from closing. I was told that the dilating exercises were critical, especially in the early months.

On February 8, we arrived at the clinic around 7:30 a.m. and met Dr. Lyle on the second floor, in the procedure office. He told Brenda and me that the surgery for breast implants would take a couple of hours, and that they would wheel me out after the procedure. I had been shown some sample implants days before and had already selected the size I felt would be appropriate for my frame.

After prepping me for surgery, Dr. Lyle held up the implants and double-checked that they were the size I wanted. I signed off on them, was sedated, and went in for the procedure. When I woke up, I had two gorgeous breasts and a small hose hanging from the incision area.

"Caisie, you're ready to go home now, and you'll need to be careful with that drainage hose. Brenda's already agreed to be your nurse, and she'll need to empty the liquid twice a day for the next two or three days. After that, she'll pull the hose out and the small incision will close on its own. Any questions?" said Doctor Lyle.

"No, Doctor. I feel fine, and wow, I look great!" I said.

"Okay, okay. We'll see you next week," Dr. Lyle chuckled.

I got into a wheelchair and Brenda wheeled me out to our car. I felt fine and was quite able to walk, but those were clinic requirements. Once we were home, I took my shirt off and gently jumped up and down, saying, "Look Brenda, look. I have boobies. Beautiful boobies."

"Caisie Breen. You stop that! You just had surgery. Do you want to open your incisions? My goodness," Brenda said.

She was right, of course. I was still doped up on pain pills and that, along with the thrill of having my first "boob" experience, was just the right combination to make me happily stupid. Fortunately, I didn't do any damage and decided to sleep the rest of my silliness off. After a few days had passed and all the swelling had gone down, I needed a 38DD bra. I was very satisfied with that.

On February 15, Brenda and I arrived at the clinic at 5:30 a.m. while the morning darkness still covered the city. I felt a certain eeriness when we arrived that had nothing to do with being nervous about the procedure. We were early and ended up waiting half an hour before the clinic staff got there. The small lobby was open, however, so we didn't have to wait outside in the cold. Pushing the elevator button was to no avail as it was still off from the night before. We sat on the cold unyielding steel benches and waited. When the staff arrived, we went up the elevator with them and into the area where Brenda would wait.

I followed an assistant to a surgical preparation room where I disrobed and put on a paper surgical gown. When I was ready, my doctor came in and explained the procedure. With his surgical cap on snugly and his mask hanging loosely from the side of his face, he said, "Hi, Caisie. Are you ready? This is going to be a far more complicated surgery than last time."

"I've never been more ready, Doc," I said.

The doctor looked at his assistant and said, "Let's go."

They wheeled me into the same cold procedure room where my breast augmentation had been performed. Once past the door, they lifted me off the gurney and laid me on the surgical table. The doctor's assistant was a large guy, with brown curls poking out of his surgical cap. I was a bit surprised to see another male assistant.

"Hello, Caisie. I'm Eric, your anesthesiologist. I'm going to be putting you to sleep in just a minute, and I'll have you do a countdown from ten to one for me. Although I must tell you, most people never make it to one. Do you have any questions before I start?"

"No. Go ahead."

I started the countdown and was out before I got to eight.

"Caisie, Caisie, are you awake?" said Eric.

Although I was almost awake, I felt like I had been on a bender and was woozy and dizzy as hell. "Yes. I guess."

"Everything went well. We're going to wheel you down to your car, and Brenda will take you on home. You're going to continue feeling a little woozy a while longer, but don't worry. It'll go away before you know it," said Doctor Lyle.

Woozy indeed. My head hurt, and I was dizzy. I almost fell over when I tried to get into the car. *Wow, that was different,* I thought.

At home, Brenda helped me into the house and into bed. I had enough pain pills to keep me in good spirits and was connected to a catheter so I didn't have to get up to pee.

Doctor Lyle showed up after three days to remove the packing. I don't know what was more disgusting—the stench or the actual site of the surgery. He helped me clean up and gave me a set of dilators. There were four, ranging in sizes from 0.675 to 1.25 inches in diameter. He instructed me to dilate with the smaller one first for fifteen minutes, then the next size up for fifteen minutes, and so on until I had the largest one in for fifteen minutes. The schedule required me to dilate three times a day for the first three months, then twice a day and decreasing in frequency until after one year, I would be down to one dilating exercise a week for maintenance.

Dilating three times a day at the beginning was incredibly taxing on my schedule. I really couldn't go anywhere for any length of time, and if I did, I had to have my tools with me and make sure I had privacy and a bed. But I made it work to the best of my ability.

By summer, however, the dilating had become painful and hard to complete. I contacted Dr. Lyle, who told me to dilate more. I followed his instructions and lengthened my dilating exercises according to the pain. The more it hurt, the longer I would dilate as those seemed to be the doctor's instructions. That wasn't the normal course of action, and later it would become much worse.

CHAPTER TWENTY-TWO

That summer of 2013, we attended another PSI contractors' convention in Boca Raton. I was looking forward to it, even though the last time I had been in Florida was when I came out to everyone by wearing a slinky cocktail dress and makeup, and that drunken contractor harassed me. Since then, many things had changed. My ID had been changed, my hair was much longer, and my muscle and fat mass had totally redistributed. I had an hourglass figure and the strength of a middle-aged woman. And surprisingly, despite taking all the voice lessons and then forgetting about them, I found my pitch was higher.

Of course, I would have to dilate while we were there, and I was worried that something might go wrong. The pain from dilating was getting worse. At home, there was no one to hear me if I screamed. I would have to double up on my pain pills and hope for the best.

Packing for the trip was easier than before, since I didn't have to pack men's clothes. Because I had to pack my dilators, I was a little concerned about the treatment I might get going through security. The dilators were an unusual shape, and I could see them getting stopped going through X-ray.

We arrived at PDX two hours before our flight. At the security check, we took off our shoes and laid our luggage on the conveyor belt to be X-rayed. When my suitcase began to go through, the security guard reversed the belt to get a better look. *Oh crap!* I thought. *Here we go.*

"Excuse me. Who does this suitcase belong to?" he asked.

"That's mine," I said.

He grabbed it. "Please follow me, ma'am." He took a couple of steps away from the line, but he was still in total view of the public as he rummaged through and found my dilators. He pulled them out and asked, "What are these, ma'am?"

My eyes began to water. I didn't know what to do. People were watching, and surely others weren't as clueless as he was. I was waiting, nearly holding my breath, for someone to start laughing. In order to avoid a further scene, I leaned in and whispered, "I am a male-to-female transgender woman, and those are my dilators."

With that, he held them up once more and said, "Oh."

I repacked everything and went through to meet up with Brenda. I was proud of myself. Although I came close, I didn't cry in front of everyone that time. I guess I was becoming more accustomed to public humiliation.

We arrived in Boca Raton later that evening, checked into the hotel, and registered for our weekly events before heading to our room to get some sleep.

"Wow, sweetie. Did you notice that?" I said.

"Notice what, dear? I didn't notice anything," Brenda said.

"Exactly." I smiled at her. "We passed hundreds of other members on the way to our room, and no one gave me a second look. And Steve and Donna, bless their hearts, they were so quick to come up and greet us with a hug. Things are indeed different from the last time we were in Florida. I'm being treated just like I was years before I came out."

"Things have changed a lot since our last trip here, and look at you," she said. "You've changed a bunch." She turned off the lights in the room. "I think we're going to have a wonderful time here, sweetie."

Unlike my last trip to Florida, when I made my announcement with over two thousand contractors present and ended up getting stalked and verbally abused, everyone accepted and treated me no differently from Brenda. The few who knew my past didn't care, and the rest simply saw me as another beautiful woman.

"Oh, look. There's the Acme booth," said Brenda.

The room was filled to near capacity, and it was elbow-to-elbow no matter what direction we wanted to go. And women definitely were at a disadvantage, as 99 percent of the room was filled with large, burly men.

"Hey, honey, come on. I found a spot," I said after wiggling my way through several big guys. At the Acme counter, the salesperson was talking about one of their latest faucets, with only two contractors looking on. After a few minutes, when he paused, I held up a finger and said, "Excuse me, sir. I have a question."

Silence. After a minute that seemed like an hour, he looked away from Brenda and me and struck up a conversation with a plumbing contractor from Texas.

"Hey, Bob. How are things in Waco?"

"I'm all right. Say, you got any of those Pimco recirc pumps I saw advertised?"

"Absolutely. Just check with me after the show. We'll getcha all fixed up."

"Brenda, I can't goddamn believe what I just saw," I said. "He was done talking with those other guys."

"Well, sweetie," Brenda said, "you really have arrived. How does this part of womanhood feel? These vendors are here to get the big contracts, and when they see you and me, they see somebody's wife." She hesitated for a moment. "The only thing that surprises me is that he was such an obvious asshole in the way he outright ignored you. Usually they will at least ask if your husband is with you. I get this all the time."

"Okay, sweetie. Watch this." Once I saw the Texas bighorn was leaving, I placed my hand on the vendor's forearm and said in a soft but crisp voice, "Hello. My name is Caisie Breen. My partner," I nodded toward my sweetie and took my hand off his arm, "is Brenda Casey. We're the owners of Casey's Plumbing in Portland, Oregon."

That got his full attention. We took home more information on tankless water heaters than we were ever able to use. Brenda was so correct. When it came to our trades, it was still a man's world. And at the vendor shows, especially in the deep South, if you're a woman, unless you wink a sultry wink or place your hand on a hairy arm for some attention, you'll probably end up a simple spectator.

When we returned home, we were happy to see that everything was in order, and there were no party leftovers like last time. There was a piece of mail on the counter that Brandon had set aside that looked like a solicitation from an organization called Our House. The card said it was a service to those with advanced stages of HIV/AIDS who were having difficulty managing independent living. It was sent by someone hosting a dinner to raise funds and awareness for the program. The food and setting were going to be Hawaiian.

I picked up the mailer and handed it to Brenda, saying, "Hey, dear. Check this out. Sounds like a fun night out, and we could support a good cause at the same time. What do you think?"

She looked it over carefully and said, "You're right. It is a great cause and Hawaiian? Count me in."

The next morning, I called and made a commitment for us. The dinner was two weeks away. We assured each other that we had plenty of time to decide what to wear to fit the Hawaiian theme.

Two weeks passed more quickly than expected, and we hadn't picked out costumes for our Hawaiian event.

"Hey, Brenda Sweet. What are we going to do to for our dinner tonight? I haven't picked anything out to wear. Have you?" I said.

"No worries, honey," Brenda said. "Remember my birthday party last year? Remember the theme?"

"That's right. It was Hawaiian, and we still have our leis. We're ready," I said.

"By the way, honey, how will we announce ourselves? I mean, do I call you my partner, my wife—any thoughts?

"Gee, I guess I haven't thought about that a lot," I said. I then got sidetracked with a phone call and forgot about her question.

That night, we arrived at the venue in our Hawaiian attire and walked up a flat-stone stairway where each stone had been hand-placed, then up a soft rolling hill that opened into the front yard. We walked over a small bridge overlooking a blue-green pond filled with large koi, which led to a path with Hawaiian torches on both sides.

Guests roamed and chatted, both inside the house and in the table-filled yard where the dinner would take place. Brenda and I decided to go inside and mingle when all of a sudden it hit me. For the first time ever, I was in a large group of gays and lesbians, as a guest. Up until then, I was totally comfortable and didn't feel out of place at all, but what if someone recognized me as a former leader of OCA?

"Hey, honey, let's go downstairs," Brenda said. She pointed to a narrow staircase at the opposite end of the room. At the bottom stood two men who were apparently having a private conversation.

"Oh, I'm sorry," I said, embarrassed. "We didn't mean to interrupt. We'll leave."

"Don't be silly," one of them answered. "We were just chatting and waiting for dinner. I'm Chad, and this is my partner, Mike."

"My name is Caisie Breen," I said with a smile, "and this is my wife, Brenda." If we couldn't feel comfortable as two married women at a gay-friendly fundraiser, then where could we? We talked with Chad and Mike for a while, and I was relieved to find that they were totally accepting.

We heard some Hawaiian music upstairs. It sounded live, and it sounded good.

"Brenda Sweet, let's go see what's going on," I said.

Brenda led the way. In the dinner area, we walked by someone playing a ukulele, someone else playing a Hawaiian drum, and two women in grass skirts singing and dancing a hula.

About halfway through dinner, as happens with most fundraisers, the host began a presentation on Our House, talking about what it was and how we could help. Brenda and I were impressed with the work and were glad to help in our own small way. But for me, there was something else going on. It was a new beginning. I had been able to get out and experience so many things that year as my full-time authentic self. And at that Hawaiian dinner, I was among friendly peers.

People just like me, beautiful people who enjoyed music, dance, and great food—I felt the same kind of camaraderie I used to feel at church. Brenda and I were glad we could be involved in Our House's ministry.

CHAPTER TWENTY-THREE

"Mama, take this badge off of me
I can't use it anymore
It's gettin' dark, too dark to see
I feel like I'm knockin' on heaven's door"

Bob Dylan

I could still smell the liquid plastic I'd used earlier in the day to modify a small vaginal lubricating injector. It was only a quarter of an inch in diameter, but I had become so small that none of the medical stents worked anymore. I had to make do with whatever I could find to remain open. I was determined to take the largest size possible, and by dipping the quarter-inch injector into liquid plastic, I was able to handle a 0.3-inch homemade stent. As I lay on my bed preparing for the ninety-minute grueling torture session, I silently prayed that I'd be able to get through it without stopping this time.

The dilating exercises became a traumatic nightmare. Eventually, Dr. Lyle had me come in for an examination. It was clear that his earlier instructions to just dilate more were not working.

When I sat down in the room in which my orchi was performed, I said, "It's been hell. I'm getting smaller and smaller, and dilating more hasn't helped. The pain is so bad that I can't even get through a session without pain pills."

"Well, you know, if you're not planning to have sex, you could just let it close—no big deal," he said.

I was stunned at his comment and told him that sex or no sex, I wanted a fully functioning vagina. He left me alone to put on a gown, then came back in and said, "Okay, Caisie, I need you to lean way back and spread your legs. I know this is going to hurt a little, but I need to get a look inside."

He didn't mince words; it did hurt like hell when he had to use a small speculum to examine me.

"Wow, I've never seen so much scar tissue. I can remove it now if you want," he said.

I didn't know the ramifications of that statement, and given the pain I was in, it wouldn't have mattered anyway. I gave the go-ahead.

"All right, Caisie, I'm going to give you a few locals, and this will sting at first. Then I'll come back in twenty minutes, and we'll see what we can do."

I still wasn't clear as to how he was going to make my dilating easier, but when he came back into the room, it was clear: he was about to carve me open like coring an apple. And although I was numb enough that the initial pain wasn't too bad, when the numbness subsided, the pain set in. Two days later, it was so great I could barely walk, but I needed to continue dilating.

One afternoon in November, as I lay on my bed with the dilator in, I heard the annoying sound of a large housefly buzz by my head. When I attempted to slap it away, my dilator fell out and landed with a thump on the floor. I lay back, defeated and nauseous, my hands shaking.

"Oh my God. Caisie!" said Brenda, running into the room and trying to keep her composure. "This just isn't going to work anymore. You've got to see a different doctor."

She was right. What I had gone through that year was nothing less than torture. After some serious Internet searching, I came across a doctor by the name of Toby Meltzer in Scottsdale, Arizona. He had strong credentials to perform what I apparently needed—a revision surgery, which would involve taking a skin graft from somewhere on my body and reforming my vagina.

When I made the trip to see him in December, he said, "Caisie, you have some serious issues that are incredibly complicated to correct."

The Charlie Brown effect kicked in. After hearing him say, "serious issues that are incredibly complicated to correct," all I heard was, "whaw, whaw, whaw, whaw."

"Serious issues that are incredibly complicated to correct?" I asked.

"Oh, relax, Caisie," Dr. Meltzer answered. "I do these all the time. But they *are* complicated, and right now, there are no guarantees. The first thing you'll need to do back home is get a CAT scan of your pelvis to make sure it will accommodate the new depth—and, of course, we'll need a cardiac clearance.

If those things come back good, I don't see any problem at all moving forward. We can probably get you in for the procedure in May."

"What about my dilating, Dr. Meltzer? The pain is off the charts, and as you can see, I'm almost closed."

"Oh, Caisie. I know it's tough, but you have to give me something to work with."

That was mixed news. It was wonderful that I would once and for all be done with all the cutting, but the thought of having to continue torturing myself was almost enough to make my heart stop. And then there was the cost of surgery: twenty thousand dollars. I didn't have that kind of money.

I went over everything Dr. Meltzer told me with Brenda once I got home.

"Wow. That is a lot of money. Did he say anything about your last surgery? I mean, what happened? Why are we doing this again?" Brenda asked.

"He wouldn't come right out and say that the other doctor screwed up, but he did say that these procedures, done successfully, always require a skin graft. I didn't get one with my other surgery."

"Caisie, honey, we can't have you go on in such pain. I want you to do whatever it takes to correct this. Can't we find the money somewhere?"

"Well, what about my retirement account? How would you feel if I borrowed the money from that?"

"Do it, honey," she said.

I had come so far. I had gone through so much hellish pain—pain that most people could never imagine, let alone endure. I had to press on; I simply had to. And as horrific as it was, I continued my dilating schedule and borrowed the money from my retirement account. I paid for the surgery in advance.

CHAPTER TWENTY-FOUR

I went into the New Year full of hope and anticipation for my final surgery. I continued my daily routine and began to count down the days to my May procedure.

Things were pretty much on cruise control at the shop. I had no reason to go there anymore, and what attention it did need, I handled from my home office. Brenda still went in to help dispatch and manage daily activities, and I took care of her at home by doing the cooking and cleaning. If it weren't for the grueling pain, I'm sure I would have enjoyed my free time more, but I tried to make the best of things and took every opportunity to have fun and feel the joy of womanhood.

By March, it was again time for one of our out-of-town contractor meetings in Dallas. Although I had been out and well-received for a long time, there was something, the same thing that kept me in the closet and repressed most of my life, lingering in my soul. I was still fearful of being in public. I needed these events for confirmation. I needed to continue sightseeing, shopping, and living my life publicly, as the woman I was, until I could finally feel safe in both body and spirit. For many of us, coming out later in life and settling into our new identities simply takes longer, and we need constant affirmation.

I was now comfortable packing women's clothing, and the process was simpler than it had been on previous trips. Though the dilating stents I'd been using were barely the size of a pencil, I took them along. *At least these won't excite the TSA*, I thought as I tucked them into my luggage.

When Brenda and I arrived at our hotel in Texas, everything went as smoothly as could be. No one treated me differently, or even seemed to remember the old me. I was smiling as we walked into our room.

"Okay, hun," I said, "What's to do? Made any plans to see the sights?"

"Not this time, sweetie. I thought we could just do some leisurely window shopping here in the hotel."

"That's cool with me. Hey, why don't we fix ourselves up and go out for a stroll?"

"Sure. Let's do it."

We got dressed, grabbed our purses, and proceeded to the hotel lobby. There were clothing shops, gift shops, and food courts—plenty to keep us interested. We strolled the long, spacious hallway toward the shops, and I could smell sweet pastries and freshly brewed coffee. As we got closer to the retail shopping area, I spotted the source of the enticing scents: the gift shop.

I couldn't pass the wonderful aroma by, so we went in and found fresh pastries and coffee. Brenda checked out the gifts while I checked out the donuts. When I heard a faint-sounding song playing behind the counter, I noticed that the young cashier had failed to turn off his iPod, and it was on the counter with music coming through the ear buds. And though it was hard to make out, the song playing sounded like Aerosmith's "Dream On." I loved that song, but there was something different about this version.

"Hi. Hey," I said to the cashier. "I couldn't help hear your music on the iPod. Is that Aerosmith's 'Dream On'?"

"Um, well, some of it," he said. "It's Eminem's 'Sing for the Moment.'"

"I love the sound; may I listen to it?" I asked.

"Well, um, I mean, there's bad language..."

"I'm an adult. No worries," I said as I took the buds from him. I listened to the song, and yep, there was bad language. It was the very music I used to abhor: rap! But I listened and listened, and I loved it. I understood every word. I almost ended up making a fool of myself by getting too much into it, but I gave the ear buds back and took note to get the song for my collection later. I'm sure the poor cashier thought he was dealing with a leftover, flower-power hippie who was probably tripping. But, no, he was dealing with an enlightened music enthusiast on a quest for new sounds.

On the final morning of the conference, at which I was well received and respected by everyone, Brenda and I waited in the hotel lobby for a cab. I looked around at the other attendees waiting with us. Brenda and I had been members of this organization for ten years, and memories of previous trips flooded my mind. Just five years earlier, a very nervous Bill Casey had walked down those hotel hallways, scared to death that someone might notice the bra he was wearing under his suit. A year later, I was afraid they would notice I was wearing light makeup. Although they didn't know it, my gradual transformation had taken place right before their eyes, right up to the day I made my announcement and was shunned by an old friend and harassed by a drunken contractor. But on that day, Brenda and I stood as equals among friends—friends who had come to accept me for who I was.

Back home, I found that one of our office windows had been broken. I had a long history as a builder and could repair just about anything. But after my transition, I gave all my tools away. Most in the transgender community continue on in their chosen profession, blue-collar or otherwise. So there I was, faced with a minor repair I should have been able to do in an hour. And yet, the thought of using a tool again made my stomach turn. It reminded me of my macho days. I finally relented and decided to just do it, rather than shell out the big bucks to hire someone else. I went to Home Depot to have a piece of glass cut.

"Hello, ma'am. How can I help you?" asked the salesperson.

"Oh, hi. I need a piece of single-glaze glass cut to these dimensions," I said, handing him my scribbled-on piece of paper.

"Let's see. Okay, no problem. Follow me."

I followed him to the back of the store and watched as he carefully set a large piece of glass on his cutting board. With two swoops, he cut it and said, "Who's going to put this in for you?"

"I was thinking about doing it myself."

"Seriously? Have you ever set glass before?"

"As a matter of fact, I have."

"Oh. Well, if you need any help, there are a few how-to brochures next to the checkouts."

Over the years, I had jacked my house up off the ground and built a full daylight basement. Later, I went on to build a two-story, three-bedroom house on top of that same house. In the years it took me to do all that, I purchased much of my material from this same Home Depot, and this young man wondered if I was up to a small window repair. I wasn't at all angry, though; in fact, I was amused. After all, he was simply seeing a "helpless, middle-aged woman," and had no idea of my earlier history. And if that's what people were seeing in me, I could live with that.

I took the glass back to the shop and completed the repair in less than an hour. Brenda decided to come out and inspect my handiwork.

"Well, well. Look at that. You've still got the touch, honey. Are you sure you don't want to wear your tool belt anymore? We sure could use another…"

"Don't you even think it," I interrupted. "I didn't want to do this repair, but it was so small, I felt, 'what the heck.'"

"Oh, I know. I was just kidding," she said.

My disdain for using tools was strictly personal. Indeed, some of the best craft people out there are female. I had begun using tools professionally as a machinist when I was much younger. I was terrible at it and ultimately changed trades. And although I learned to use plumbing and other construction tools proficiently, I was always getting injured and/or cut. I just wasn't going to expose my body to that anymore.

May finally came, and my surgery was all paid for. My pelvis had been screened to ensure there was proper depth, and I had my cardiac clearance. We would be in Scottsdale for ten days. My surgery would be on the morning after I arrived, and I'd remain in the clinic, recovering, for three days. Then, I would be under the care of my Brenda Sweet for another six days of recovery at a motel before finally returning home.

"Hey, honey. Are you looking forward to this trip?" I asked. "I know it's a long one."

"Seriously? Do you have any idea what it's been like seeing you go through so much pain? Honey, I love you so much. And I'm so looking forward to you having a normal, pain-free life again. So yes, I'm looking forward to it," Brenda replied.

"Aww. That's so sweet, honey. I know all this has been hard on you too. Thanks for standing by me. I love you so much," I said as we embraced.

We arrived in Scottsdale on May 6, 2014. The clinic was a beautiful building just off the main highway. We made our way to the second-floor office where my surgery would take place the following morning and proceeded to the sign-in window.

"Good morning, Ms. Breen. Tomorrow's your big day. Are you all ready?" asked the check-in attendant.

"Absolutely! I've been ready for months," I said.

"Oh, I completely understand. You're in good hands now. We're going to take very good care of you. Remember, no solids after 10 tonight and no liquids after 4 a.m. You'll need to be here at 7 a.m., and you're scheduled for surgery at 9 a.m. Any questions?"

"None at all. I'm ready!" I said.

"Very well, then. We'll see you in the morning."

I woke up early the next day, full of anticipation and just a little nervous. Although I was very confident in Dr. Meltzer, I had been through so much at that point, I couldn't help wonder if it would work this time. *Will I finally have a body that matches my mind?*

After I was admitted, a nurse greeted me. "Good morning, Caisie Breen. Here is your hospital gown. You can give Brenda what you're wearing to take with her. You won't be needing anything for a few days."

"Oh, sure," said Brenda. "Here, Caisie. Just put your things in my bag. I won't be going anywhere until after your surgery, but I'll take them with me when I do."

After I put my gown on, I was wheeled into a waiting room just outside the surgery. After a brief wait, Dr. Meltzer came in dressed in scrubs. With a beautiful smile, he said, "Well, Caisie, today's your day. How do you feel?"

"I've never felt better, Dr. Meltzer. I am so ready!" I answered.

"I'm sure you are, Caisie. As I said earlier, this is going to be a complicated procedure, and you'll be under for at least five hours. Do you have any questions before we begin?"

"None at all. Let's go!"

I woke up late that afternoon feeling tingly from head to toe. I had tears of happiness in my eyes as I scanned the room for my Brenda Sweet. I saw her reading just outside my room, next to a hospital window. "Hi, honey," I said, trying to force my dry mouth into a smile.

She looked up at me with a grin and said, "Oh, sweetie, you're awake! How do you feel?"

"They've done a great job with the meds, so I'm feeling pretty good, thank you," I said.

My experience with Dr. Meltzer was so different from my previous surgeries. There were no pain issues at any time, and my care both before and after was superb. Brenda spent the night with me that first night, and for the next two days, she came in the morning and left at dinnertime.

On the day I was to be discharged, Dr. Meltzer came to my room to see me off.

"How are you feeling Caisie?

"Pretty good Dr . Meltzer. Thanks."

"Wonderful. Well, your surgery was a great success and you shouldn't have any more pain issues going forward. So are you ready to get out of here?"

"Yes I am. And thank you and your staff, for the excellent care. You guys are wonderful!"

"Well thank you Caisie. We do try."

Dr Meltzer, before I leave, I have to ask you—why, why do you choose to do these kind of procedures?"

"Well Caisie, I've found that those in the transgender community are always so appreciative of what I can do for them. It brings me joy and fulfillment to help them become who they want to be."

Then just before he left, he did the sweetest thing: he gave me a warm embrace, laying his head on my shoulder.

I spent the next several days in our motel, recovering before we flew home. Dr. Meltzer's nurse removed the surgical packing the day I left the clinic, and I began a new dilating schedule.

At home, everything seemed fresh and new. Gone were the smells of liquid plastic and the dilating sessions that seemed to never end. Dr. Meltzer had prescribed fifteen minutes at a time, and that was all it took. And best of all, there was no more pain.

The day after our return was a meeting day with our plumbers and electricians. I decided to show up for a visit. It had been a long time since I'd attended an office meeting. Even though by then I was well accepted and no longer a novelty, I was still nervous. I had changed. My hair was much longer, I had learned to carry myself as a woman in the way I walked, and the pitch of my voice was a bit higher.

When Brenda and I pulled into the driveway of our shop, the sun was just rising, and the view looked like a scene on a spring postcard. And though we arrived a few minutes early, everyone else was already seated, apparently waiting for something. There was the usual smell of freshly brewed hot coffee, and someone had brought donuts. As I entered the meeting room, I heard:

"Hi, Caisie."

"Hey, Caisie. Good to see you!"

"Well, hello, stranger!"

Almost all of them had known me before my change. All were blue-collar tradespeople who, in most cultures, would faint being around people like me at best, and outright reject me at worst. And yet there they were, giving me what felt like a hero's welcome. I did my best to keep my eyes dry as I shook some hands and engaged in conversation. I felt free from the fear that had kept me away from the office earlier. Finally, I was at peace.

Brenda was surprised, too. As the new manager, she was initially nervous about me showing up at the meetings. It demonstrated to both of us that we had a wonderful, mature, and loyal team of workers, and that I must have done something right along the way for them to show me such kindness.

The following Sunday I spent the morning cleaning house and getting ready for our Sunday family dinner. I had my music on a little louder than usual. Brenda was out and I was alone, so I cranked it up. I had just discovered Metallica and was rocking out to "Nothing Else Matters." I'd heard it for the first time on YouTube and couldn't believe I was digging it so much—another metal band I had cursed in the past. I turned it up loud enough to hear over the vacuum cleaner, and I danced as well as I could while cleaning. As loud as it was, though, it didn't drown out the knock on the back door. Brandon had moved into our downstairs apartment.

"Hold on, I'm coming," I yelled as I turned my music off and ran to the back door. "Hi, son. C'mon in. What's up?"

"I heard the loud music," he said, "and thought there must be a party or something. And do you know who that was you were listening to?"

"Um, Metallica?" I replied.

"Since when have you listened to them? You used to chastise me for listening to them."

"I know. Weird, huh? I can't really explain it, son. For some time now, my taste in music has been totally crazy. I not only dig this one, but check it out, I've even found some Eminem rap tunes I absolutely love. Amazing, I know. But things have changed. And my appetite for good sound has changed a lot," I said.

"Oh, well. As long as you're happy. By the way, what are we having for dinner tonight?" he asked.

"Baked spaghetti. Can you be here at five?" I replied.

"See ya then," he said.

Before Ryan came over for dinner, I needed to make a run to the store. I checked the fridge to see what I needed. I saw a salad and decided I was hungry. I grabbed a large bowl, the vinaigrette dressing, and a fork, and went to the dining room to feast. There was something special about that salad. It looked like the monster salad I'd made during Aunt Becky's beach retreat. And the smell of my homemade salad dressing reminded me of taking on the cooking at home.

It had been such a remarkable journey. I'd done the twist with my sister as a child in one of her dresses, only to be told it was wrong for boys to wear dresses. I'd had the honor and privilege of seeing Aretha Franklin perform "Respect" in person at a time when I didn't have a clue who she was. I thought about more recent events, like the feeling of loss I had when watching my firstborn move away. And color—my discovery of color was absolutely surreal.

And of course the other biggies—music, the supernatural sound overhaul within me. And Tia saying, "What's it going to be, Bill?" Brenda saying, "You are a woman!" Such a long, fantastic journey, with so many people affected. And almost everyone had grown to love and accept the new me. I had so much to be thankful for.

"Okay, everyone. Five o-clock, dinnertime." I said.

"Hey, Ryan. Please pass the potatoes. By the way, how's your computer coming?" I said.

Ryan passed me the potatoes and said, "Great! I'm glad you asked. I only need a five-gig memory card to get it done."

"I've got one I'll sell you cheap," Brandon said.

"Thanks," said Ryan. "That'll really help."

"Hey, guys. I just picked up a song on YouTube by Coldplay called "Paradise." Have either of you heard it? I absolutely love it!" I said.

"Oh, yeah. Me too," Brandon replied.

"Sure. Love it," said Ryan.

"What do you think, Mom? Have you heard it?" Brandon asked.

"Oh, you guys know I don't follow that music," Brenda replied.

Ryan, Brandon, and I laughed and continued eating and making great memories. Indeed, our Sunday dinner was exactly like every other Sunday dinner the Casey family had enjoyed together. We loved each other dearly, and it didn't matter that it was now Caisie Breen preparing the meals. Our dinner conversation was still warm, with us asking the boys what they'd been up to and them giving heartfelt responses— and with Ryan, of course, adding a little humor.

My life had returned to normal, and I was more determined than ever to spend the rest of it being a blessing to others, in the same way my dear Grandma Grace was up to the day she left the world.

AFTERWORD

Spring, 2016

I still live in Portland with Brenda. We don't belong to any organized religion, and I am registered politically as an Independent. I am semi-retired and still spend much of my time writing and interacting on Facebook. Since beginning this book, my Songbyrd group has grown, along with my appetite for new sounds. The new artists and songs my friends have turned me onto have been priceless. Only recently my sweet friend Krystine introduced me to 2Cellos, a Croatian duo. I couldn't believe their sound, and spent days savoring their renditions of everything from hard rock to soft classical.

During the period I was writing this book, awareness about the lives of trans people was exploding through such programs as *I am Cait*, *Transparent*, and *Girls, Inc.* And though this has certainly brought us closer to mainstream acceptance, it has also brought out those who will not accept us and see violence as their only recourse when coming face to face with us. Twice as many of us were murdered in 2015 than in 2014.

There is diversity within the trans community, and not all male-to-females have the same need for a complete sexual realignment surgery, like I did. Those identifying as the gender they believe their brain dictates should be honored and respected whether they've had surgeries or not. I don't even use the term "trans" anymore in relation to myself. I am a woman: physically, mentally, and emotionally.

As society continues to go through these growing pains, my fervent prayer is that we in the trans community remain hand in hand as peacemakers—first to love and first to forgive. And I hope that ultimately, society as a whole will embrace all those in the trans community, and that silly things like who can use what bathroom will become a thing of the past.

~ end ~

Bibliography

Ballard, Henry "Hank". <u>The Twist</u>

Lennon, John and McCartney, Paul. <u>I Want to Hold Your Hand.</u>

Hendrix, Jimi. <u>Purple Haze</u>

Robinson, William. <u>Get Ready</u>

Hazelwood, Lee. <u>These Boots are Made for Walking</u>

Lennon, Johm and McCartney, Paul. <u>She Loves You.</u>

Simon, Paul. <u>The Sound of Silence.</u>

Thompson, Wayne. <u>Letter</u>

Phillips, John. <u>San Francisco (Be Sure to Wear Some Flowers in Your Hair).</u>

DuBoff, Stephen. and Kornfeld, Arthur. <u>The Rain, the Park and Other Things.</u>

Lennon, John and McCartney, Paul. <u>I Saw Her Standing There</u>

McCartney, Paul. <u>Motor of Love.</u>

Berry, Bill; Buck, Peter; Mills, Michael; and Stipe, Michael. <u>It's the End of the World as We Know It (And I Feel Fine).</u>

McVie, Christine. <u>Songbird.</u>

Greenwood, Charles; Greenwood, Richard Guy; Hammond,
  Albert; Hazelwood, Michael; O'Brien, Edward;
  Selway, Philip; and York, Thomas. <u>Creep.</u>

Lennon, John and McCartney, Paul. <u>She Loves You.</u>

Lennon, John and McCartney, Paul. <u>Good Day Sunshine.</u>

Dylan, Bob. <u>Knocking on Heaven's Door.</u>

Gaye, Marvin; Hunter, Ivy Jo; and Stevenson, William.
  <u>Dancing in the Streets.</u>